FROM POWER TO PARTNERSHIP

Britain in the Commonwealth
The Church of England in the Anglican Communion

Report of the International and Development Affairs Committee of the Board for Social Responsibility

CHURCH HOUSE PUBLISHING
Church House, Great Smith Street, London SW1P 3NZ

ISBN 0 7151 6576 3

Published 1991 for the General Synod Board for Social Responsibility by Church House Publishing

This report has only the authority of the Board by which it was prepared

Printed in England by Rapier Press Ltd

CONTENTS

ACKNOWLEDGEMENTS

We wish to acknowledge the many people who gave generously of their time and expertise in interview, writing and comment. Without their assistance the report would have been the poorer.

Special thanks go to the (then) Archbishop of Canterbury, the (then) Secretary-General of the Commonwealth, Lord Moore, Lord Briggs, Canon Sam Van Culin, Margaret Jeffery, Simon Longstaff and Sir Peter Marshall.

FOREWORD

When is Britain finally going to adjust to the reality that it is no longer an imperial power and to start belonging to the rest of the world as a genuinely interdependent partner? How are the British government and people going to develop a new and integral relationship with the Commonwealth at the same time as they genuinely take their place in a new Europe?

These are critical questions confronting the British nation. Parallel questions face all the Churches in Britain. Here perhaps a supreme example is the Church of England. How can the former 'Mother Church' now discover a newly receptive commitment to the rest of the Anglican Communion?

How can we all in this country take our whole international past, duly redeemed through an honest and searching reappraisal, into an increasingly European future?

Such questions have been both obscured and intensified in recent years by certain stressful and divisive issues, symptoms of the difficulty church and nation alike experience in coming to terms with the search for new patterns in human society, a new kind of international order. One such issue across the whole Anglican Communion has been the ordination of women; for the Commonwealth another division, more particularly cutting Britain off from the other members, has been South Africa.

But the crucial requirement for Britain and for the Churches alike is as this report states 'by accepting the past to alter its meaning'. On this, Britain's future identity and fulfilment and that of our Churches and people depend.

That is why this report is timely. Indeed it is the reason for its appearance. It is the reason why the International and Development Affairs Committee of the Board for Social Responsibility of the Church of England kept seeing that this work cried out to be done.

The possibility of a new phase in international affairs occurred while the Report was being prepared, through dramatic changes in East – West relationships. In other spheres leadership changed.

The Commonwealth had a new Secretary General; the Anglican

Communion a new Archbishop of Canterbury and Britain a new Prime Minister. These changes highlighted the difficulties in producing a report which attempts to analyse and assess not only history but also current events.

The members of the Working Party between them had extensive experience of the two organisations under review. Some had been born in Commonwealth countries other than Britain; others had lived and worked in other Commonwealth countries.

Our thanks are due to the Very Revd Michael Mayne and the Working Party who gave their time and effort to writing this report, and to Pamela Gruber who ensured that the process ran as smoothly as possible. Special thanks go to Becky Roberts for her skill and efficiency on the word processor.

We believe and hope that this document will enable its readers, in both the UK and beyond, to recognise and grasp the opportunity which membership of the Commonwealth – and for Christians of their World Church bodies – provides for making a vital contribution to the shaping of a new, more just and sustainable world community in the coming century.

†SIMON COVENTRY
Chairman,
International and Development Affairs Committee

MEMBERS OF THE WORKING PARTY AND ITS TERMS OF REFERENCE

Members of the Working Party

Chairman:

The Very Revd Michael Mayne	Dean of Westminster

Members:

Ms Anne Blackburn	Bankee
Mr Nadir Dinshaw	Vice-President, Joint Council for the Welfare of Immigrants
The Very Revd John Gladwin	Provost of Sheffield
Professor D. A. Low	President of Clare Hall and Smuts Professor of the History of the British Commonwealth, University of Cambridge
The Rt Revd Humphrey Taylor	Bishop of Selby (formerly Secretary of USPG)
Mrs Hazel Wright	Head Teacher, Grove Infant and Nursery School, Handsworth

Secretary:

Ms Pamela Gruber	Secretary to the International and Development Affairs Committee BSR

Terms of reference

1. To consider the place and role of the Commonwealth as a grouping of nations in international affairs and as a Commonwealth of peoples today and in the future.
2. To evaluate Britain's role as a member of the Commonwealth as this role has developed from being one of leadership to one of equal membership.
3. To offer a perspective from the Church's own membership of an international body, the Anglican Communion, on what such membership entails.

PRAYERS FOR THE COMMONWEALTH

Blessed are you, Sovereign God, ruler of nations:
to you be glory and praise for ever!
From the rising of the sun to its setting
your name is proclaimed in all the world.
In your love you made us in your image
and claim us for yourself,
the joy and crown of all creation.
When we turn from you, you do not forsake us
but in your mercy you search us out
and draw us together into union with you
as members together of one human family.
By your Spirit you renew the face of the earth,
entrusting to us the gift of creation.
By your love made perfect in human weakness
you have revealed to us your eternal purpose.
You have delivered us from the dominion of darkness
and laid open before us the paths of righteousness.
Teach us to pray and to long for your kingdom
where mercy and truth shall embrace one another
and fear and mistrust shall be no more;
where justice and peace shall spring up from the earth,
and the nations shall walk in the light of your presence.
So may the people praise you, O God,
Sovereign of all, now and for ever. **Amen.**

God of grace and God of all,
whose will is that your people should be free,
and the whole earth live to praise your name;
Call the nations you have made to cease from strife,
that we we may be united against our common foes
of want and disease, of greed and inhumanity.
Lead your people from death to life, from war to peace,
that we may build a new world of justice and righteousness.
End the dark night of ignorance and despair,
and use this Commonwealth of Nations as an instrument of your peace
to herald the dawn of your kingdom of mercy and truth;
where you live and reign, one God now and for ever. **Amen.**

PART I

The classroom was dominated by a large print entitled 'The boy scout's oath'. In it the evidently bewildered boy scout was led by the hand of Jesus, who, with his other hand, indicated a map on which the British Empire was lit by a strange, unearthly radiance.

Sir Peter Ustinov

The Commonwealth is a source of common sense in the world. It cannot negotiate on behalf of the world, but it can caution the world and help the world to negotiate.

President von Weizsäcker of Germany

Chapter 1

TUPPENCE FOR THE COMMONWEALTH

Setting the scene

1 Dear Sir, With the exception of The Queen and a handful of officials, does anyone care tuppence about the Commonwealth? Yours faithfully,
James Belmont.

That letter appeared in *The Independent* as we started our Working Party consultations. A few days later a letter from a reader in Chalfont St Giles put it even more strongly: 'The Commonwealth has become a counter-productive shambles'. Our task is not to do a public relations job for the Commonwealth, or sing its praises in unrealistic and immodest terms. Yet the burden of this Report is that such disenchanted writers are wide of the mark: not just mildly mistaken, but purblind, and plain wrong. We shall seek to show that the Commonwealth, tenuous, vulnerable, indefinable, is actually and potentially a uniquely effective model for international relationships and co-operation between nations in our changed and rapidly changing world.

2 Our brief is clear and deliberately circumscribed. It is to analyse the nature of the Commonwealth and Britain's past and present role within it, and to ask if there are lessons to be learned from the analogous membership of the Church of England within the Anglican Communion: e.g. how bodies may be both autonomous and interdependent; how communities may heal painful memories and redeem present tensions. We are well aware of the developing nature of all such international bodies. It may be that their proper destiny is ultimately to die, both to make way for something of greater value and to bring to it their own distinctive gifts; and we return to this at the end of our Report. We recognise the wider canvas: of Europe, the United Nations, other international bodies and groupings, other traditions, other Faiths, and we share a vision of a united, world-wide Church. But our brief is with Britain *in* the Commonwealth and the Church of England *in* the Anglican Communion. That the operative word is 'in' and not 'and' goes to the heart of our concern.

3 At a recent Commonwealth Conference, the Speaker of the Canadian House of Commons gave this useful analogy of how the Commonwealth should function.

> When geese migrate they fly in formation and help each other – each goose flapping its wings creates an uplift for the goose that follows. All the geese making their individual contribution give the whole flock a 70 per cent greater flying range than would be the case if each bird were to fly alone. Furthermore, when a goose begins to lag behind or get out of formation, the others 'honk' it back into position.

4 The greater part of this Report has emerged from meetings in the shadow of Westminster Abbey, a place in which the saga of Britain's changed role is perfectly expressed. For generations it has been regarded as the Mother Church, formerly of the Empire, latterly of the Commonwealth. In 1920 Dean Ryle wrote:

> Can any sacred building in the British Empire compare with Westminster Abbey? Familiar as it is to some of us, to our visitors the Abbey is the heart shrine of the worldwide Empire. The thought of it is intertwined with the most sacred feelings and deepest affection of brothers and sisters scattered over the whole world.

5 Perhaps the old Empire finds its most flowery memorial in the Abbey on the monument to William Pitt, Earl of Chatham, 'during whose Administration in the Reigns of George II and George III Divine Providence exalted Great Britain to an Height of Prosperity and Glory unknown to any former Age'. But as the Empire died and gave way to the Commonwealth, as domination was followed by co-existence, so services of dedication were held in the Abbey for new nations achieving independence and self-government. Today permanent stalls are named for High Commissioners, and on the eve of each National Day of a Commonwealth nation the High Commissioner is invited to Choral Evensong to read the New Testament lesson, and prayers are said for the nation in question.

6 On Commonwealth Day in March, the 50 Commonwealth nations come to the Abbey in the presence of HM the Queen for a multi-faith Observance. The Commonwealth flags are carried in procession by young people from each Commonwealth nation. All those present join in five affirmations which declare those basic values which unite all its members: affirmations which speak of the dignity and unique worth of every human person; the need to establish justice for every individual; the need to assert the supremacy of love in all

human relationships; our responsibility for exercising our stewardship of the natural world with care; and our membership of the one human family and our expression of it in service and sacrifice for the common good.

The Commonwealth agenda and media response

7 The members of the Commonwealth make up one-quarter of the world's population. A list of them appears at Appendix A. Thus the Commonwealth Heads of Government Meetings (para. 35ff) are an important forum for the discussion of key issues of the day. The Communiqué released at the end of each meeting indicates the wide range of topics which are discussed and the one issued after Kuala Lumpur (1989) is no exception. Comment was made on some fourteen different areas of the world where there were particular problems, ranging from Afghanistan to the Middle East. Issues which are of global concern were discussed, such as terrorism, drug abuse and illicit trafficking and the world economic situation. Environmental issues of particular concern were covered by a special declaration from Langkawi where the 'retreat' was held (para. 271).

8 Yet few would suspect this wide range of topics from the media coverage, and clearly the Commonwealth is currently out of fashion. 'The Commonwealth has little in common and no wealth' quipped Enoch Powell; and he wrote at the time of the Vancouver meeting in 1987:

> The recent happenings in Fiji, a tin-pot state on the other side of the world, have done more than years of patient reasoning to awaken the British to the nonsense of the Commonwealth and start them wondering if they hadn't better ditch the whole show after all.... The time has come to jettison a venerable piece of national self-deception which, if it ever served a useful purpose, has long outlived it.

Simon Jenkins, now Editor of *The Times*, but then writing for *The Sunday Telegraph*, weighed in under the headline 'Having it up at the Humbug Club':

> The Commonwealth is now simply a 'relationship', a 'wonderful family', a 'diverse grouping' – as if the very lack of common purpose is a virtue. Here is the proverbial body whose sole purpose is to look for a purpose .... The Institution is swiftly developing diplomatic elephantiasis to ward off the virus of irrelevance. It has spawned some two hundred and fifty subsidiary organisations... After Kuala Lumpur, the British Prime

Ministers should decline to attend meetings of this unpleasant organisation.

9 None of this is new. Shortly after the Commonwealth Heads of Government Meeting of 1969, British newspapers were demanding the Commonwealth's demise:

'The Commonwealth today has become a voice-less, vision-less collection of self-seeking states... its conferences are ever more spiteful charades ... The Commonwealth as it now exists should be wound up'. (*Daily Sketch*. But 'the dog it was that died', for the *Daily Sketch* was itself 'wound up' within a short time.) 'Few maintain any longer that this association is anything but a harmful nuisance to Britain's own interests ... Hard as it may seem, the United Kingdom would do best to withdraw from it.' (*The Daily Telegraph*)

10 The historical reasons why hostility and disillusionment exists are spelled out in Chapter 3. We believe many of the more common criticisms are misconceived. Often they are deliberate travesties. Sometimes they are made in ignorance of the facts. Some of the critics are those with predictably similar views on related subjects such as immigration and aid to developing nations. Such 'little-Englander' critics seem to imply that once a country becomes autonomous all our mutual responsibilities vanish. It is a bleak vision.

Public opinion

11 An accurate reflection of public opinion is hard to come by. In 1986 – the year of the peak of the quarrel over South African sanctions and of the boycott of the Commonwealth Games in Edinburgh – there was a Gallup Poll in the United Kingdom and Canada. In Canada three out of five people supported the Commonwealth and one-third thought it a good example of inter-racial co-operation (a fairly steep decline from the figures in a 1963 Poll). In the United Kingdom only one-quarter saw the Commonwealth as more important than the European Community or the United States, down from one-third in 1969. However, 40 per cent thought it very important that Britain had close relations with the Commonwealth, about the same percentage as for the United States. Half thought it would be 'very serious' or 'fairly serious' if the Commonwealth broke up, and there was an increase of British people who believed that the value of the association lies in bringing people of different races together.

12 In the United Kingdom support was strongest among those of 45 and over, among Labour and centrist voters, and among the unskilled. It was lowest among those under 34 and among Conservative voters. In Canada support was strongest among the university-educated, the English-speakers, women and those over 50.

Four reasons for criticism

13 Sometimes criticisms of the Commonwealth strike home. How could it be otherwise when the body in question has no constitution, imposes no statutory obligations on its members and has no executive functions? Rather it is an association of free and diverse nations who wish to consult and work together for their own and the common good. But it may be helpful in this first chapter to pin-point briefly four reasons why the Commonwealth attracts such criticism.

14 a) ITS INDEFINABLE NATURE

Because the Commonwealth is indefinable, it is a hard concept to put across in the Press. It is a politically structured arrangement that links the former largest colonial power, Britain; those former colonies that are predominantly white and affluent (Australia, Canada, New Zealand) which accept HM the Queen as monarch; and a large number of other countries which were formerly territories of the British Empire, which now have a variety of forms of government and which represent a wide cross-section of social and religious groups. It is a much more sophisticated concept than that of empire, where one country was at the centre of a colonial web. It operates on many levels, having 50 equal members while its titular head lives in Britain. At the 1987 conference of the Commonwealth Journalists' Association all were agreed that the Commonwealth was under-reported and that 'most of the criticism of the Commonwealth, particularly in the British media, is unjustified, even mischievous'.

b) ACCUSATIONS CONCERNING HUMAN RIGHTS ABUSE

15 The criticism of humbug and hypocrisy refers to racial oppression and other denials of human rights in certain Commonwealth countries. Undoubtedly a number of them have had bad human rights records: Amnesty International reports prove that. Yet of all those nations covered by Amnesty reports, 34 of the 50 Commonwealth

countries are well and fairly run parliamentary democracies, only four have military or quasi-military governments, and only six are the one-party states which some commentators find obnoxious, but which are by no means equally undemocratic. The Heads of Government in Kuala Lumpur in 1989 requested the Secretary-General to convene a governmental working group of experts on human rights within the Commonwealth. It will be reporting to the Heads of Government Meeting in Harare in October 1991. But it has to be remembered that one of the major principles of Commonwealth partnership is that each is a sovereign state and member governments do not concern themselves in the internal affairs of other member nations. It is a free association of equals, and there can be no legal obligation to take common action as a result of discussion or consensus. However, if the lack of rights in a sovereign state is in question, the matter can be discussed more easily in the Commonwealth than at the United Nations.

c) CONFLICTING LOYALTIES WITH THE EUROPEAN COMMUNITY

16 It is sometimes argued that Britain must choose between the Commonwealth and the European Community, and that loyalty to one weakens commitment to the other. From time to time Britain could use her dual membership in a negative way to argue her point of view selectively and to her advantage, especially when she found herself isolated. We recognise this temptation, but we believe that her membership of the one in fact can be used to enhance her role in the other: that Britain without the Commonwealth would be regarded as of less significance by the European Community, and that Britain's European economic links enable her to play a more constructive role in the Commonwealth. (paras 234, 235)

d) FEAR OF MULTI-CULTURAL SOCIETY

17 A key word in this Report will be interdependence, both in terms of nations and churches. Within the nation, during the last 40 years there has emerged a new multi-cultural, multi-lingual, multi-faith Britain. Nearly 2.05 million British residents are non-white, and four out of every ten non-white British citizens are citizens by birth as well as residence. Some critics blame the Commonwealth for the fact that Britain is now a multi-racial society. Despite all the tension this brings, we do not believe it to be a weakness but a strength. Our

chapter on Immigration (8) is a reminder of how great the contribution of those from the West Indies and the Indian sub-continent has been to our industry and our social and health services. We believe Britain to be richer culturally and spiritually for the contribution of its citizens who originated from the Commonwealth: richer for the spontaneous vigour and fun symbolised by the West Indian Notting Hill Carnival; the new cultural creativity seen and heard in the arts, in food and in fashion; the qualities of dignity, resilience and humour evident in many people of Asian and African origin.

Analogy with the Church of England in the Anglican Communion

18 For Anglicans there is a strangely pertinent analogy. Just under half the dioceses in the Anglican Communion are in the Commonwealth. Both the Commonwealth and the Anglican Communion have titular heads and both of them are British. HM the Queen is Head of the Commonwealth: the Archbishop of Canterbury *primus inter pares*, 'first among equals', within the Anglican Communion and Chairman of its Lambeth Conference, held every ten years.

19 Like the Commonwealth's biennial Heads of Government meetings, the Anglican Communion also has its biennial meetings of Primates. It is dangerous to draw too close a parallel between the two, but a case could be argued that Commonwealth Heads of Government and Primates have some similarities in that they are the focal points for decision-making in their countries/provinces. The Primates' meetings deal with theological, ecclesiastical, social and political issues of common concern to the Communion. One such meeting in Cyprus took place during the life of the Working Party.

20 At that meeting in May 1989, the Archbishop of Canterbury was asked by his fellow Primates to send a pastoral visit to Namibia. One purpose of the visit was to express the concern and encouragement of the Anglican Communion to the Church and people of Namibia as the process of moving towards independence began. Another one was to enable the Anglican Communion to be informed of developments during that process.

21 This ability to organise quickly and easily international groups to

undertake specific tasks is shared by both the Anglican Communion and the Commonwealth. It is noteworthy that Archbishop Edward Scott, the former Primate of Canada, was called upon to serve both the Commonwealth's Eminent Persons Group which went to South Africa and the Anglican Communion group which went to Namibia.

22 The Lambeth Conference is *sui generis* and no parallel really exists in the Commonwealth. During the life of the Working Party the twelfth Lambeth Conference was held in 1988. 28 self-governing provinces make up the Anglican Communion and, although fewer in number than the Commonwealth member states, it encompasses a wider range of countries, most notably the United States of America and those in Latin America, though in neither is the Anglican presence a large one. Attendance is by diocese. 525 bishops attended in 1988 and it lasted for 22 days. Although not a true parallel, perhaps the pastoral letters from Lambeth could be likened to the Commonwealth Heads of Government Meetings' (CHOGM) communiqué as a summation of the items discussed. Seven such letters came from the Conference covering topics addressed in smaller groupings by it. These ranged from topics concerning Anglicans, to those concerning all Christians, to those which concern the whole of humankind. Real parallels can be drawn between the global discussions at Lambeth and those at Vancouver and Kuala Lumpur.

A Commonwealth of peoples

23 If one purpose of this Report is to rebut uninformed criticism of the Commonwealth, a much more important purpose is to offer an Anglican assessment of the role of the Commonwealth in the 1990s. It is a community linked by past history and by bonds of affection which provides a context in which a number of critical issues can be addressed: issues of racism and sexism, patterns of development and environmental concerns, the gap between 'the haves and the have nots'. It has a much simpler structure than the United Nations. It can be supportive of UN initiatives, and it can also take initiatives which are not possible for the UN by being responsive to, and knowledgeable about, issues which particularly effect small states.

24 The Commonwealth is with us, a 'given' reality, and the question is whether Britain is prepared to participate in its life in a constructive way; or whether we continue to patronise it with faint praise and

marginal interest, and by under-funding its agencies. Certainly many British people are uninterested in the Commonwealth, and it is no vote-catcher. Nevertheless, the language of friendship is important, and it needs to be remembered that a huge number of families have relatives in other parts of the Commonwealth, whether it be in Australia, New Zealand or Canada, Zimbabwe or Kenya, or the West Indies, Pakistan or Bangladesh.

25 In his autobiography Lord Carrington writes that he believes the predominant indicator of relations between countries is not the opinions and comments and interchange of politicians, but the feelings of ordinary people towards ordinary people of other nations; feelings which may be 'based on myth, out-dated memory, comfortable (or hostile) illusion...'; what he calls 'the human connection'. This connection undoubtedly exists, he has written, within 'The Old Commonwealth', but also, 'in subtle, often confusing forms, between the British and those countries we once governed as aliens' (for example, the continuing relationship of Britain and India arising out of their shared and troubled past).

26 'I understand those people' writes Lord Carrington, 'who say that it is meaningless to give to the human connection an institutional form: that it fosters illusion and absurdity and actually exacerbates ill feeling. I understand, but I do not agree. It would be a bad thing if the Commonwealth were to break up. Everything evolves, develops or loses momentum, dies if wholly useless, survives and discovers new vigour if genuine need exists. We should not be over-polite, or pretend, or sentimentalise over the Commonwealth. We should not talk of it as if it were something it isn't. It is not a power bloc. It is not a preferential trading partnership as once it was. It is not an Empire. It speaks with many voices, some of them intensely provoking from time to time. Yet it consists not of governments but of peoples; and those peoples have at some period in their histories been touched by similar influences, learned from some of the same books, played some of the same games, imbibed (and sometimes neglected) comparable principles of law and administration. Fought, at least once, under the same flag. There is a human connection, not contemptible because varied, uneven and intangible... One should not abandon an institution because it is not something else, something it cannot be. I was glad to serve as both Foreign and *Commonwealth* Secretary.'

Chapter 2

THE COMMONWEALTH

27 The Commonwealth in this last decade of the twentieth century is something very different from much of its reporting in the popular press and carping criticism from some academics and others. This Chapter seeks to give a factual résumé of the Commonwealth and its institutions, and suggests its role in the global context, and its potential as a world body.

28 Over a quarter of the world's population – more than one billion people – live in the countries of the Commonwealth. Its members are to be found in every continent of the world, from very many economic and political systems. Its peoples belong to every race and religion. It is the only international grouping outside the United Nations to form such a cross-section of the world community from developed and developing countries; and one of its advantages is that it does not belong to any of the world's power blocs.

29 The Commonwealth, unlike the United Nations, has no charter and thus enjoys a unique flexibility. However at the 1971 Singapore Commonwealth Heads of Government Meeting (CHOGM) the Declaration of Commonwealth Principles was expounded as follows:

> We believe that international peace and order are essential to the security and prosperity of mankind.
>
> We believe in the liberty of the individual, in equal rights for all citizens regardless of race, colour, creed or political belief, and in their inalienable right to participate by means of free and democratic political processes in framing the society in which they live.
>
> We recognise racial prejudice as a dangerous sickness threatening the healthy development of the human race and racial discrimination as an unmitigated evil of society.
>
> We oppose all forms of colonial domination and racial oppression and are committed to the principles of human dignity and equality.
>
> We believe that the wide disparities in wealth now existing between different sections of mankind are too great to be tolerated.

We believe that international co-operation is essential to remove the causes of war, promote tolerance, combat injustice, and secure development among the peoples of the world.

30 Today's Commonwealth is the successor to the British Empire which was succeeded by the British Commonwealth. From eight countries in 1950 the membership rose to 11 in 1960, 30 in 1970 and with Namibian independence in 1990 to 50 members. The growth in membership marches with decolonisation in the former Empire. For Britain the biggest change has been from being the 'mother' country during the days of British Empire and British Commonwealth to being an equal member, albeit one held, for historic reasons, in considerable esteem. There is still much respect in the Commonwealth for Britain and British institutions.

31 A large part of this esteem comes undoubtedly from the special role that HM the Queen has played in the development of the modern Commonwealth. She has shown to its individual members that she is deeply committed to the Commonwealth as an institution and to her role as its Head. Her three sons have each spent a year in different Commonwealth countries: the Prince of Wales in Australia, Prince Andrew in Canada, Prince Edward in New Zealand. Like the Commonwealth itself, the Queen has been subjected to criticism for her devotion to it not just by the tabloid press but by what are termed quality publications such as *The Times* and *The Spectator*. She is fully aware of these criticisms of the Commonwealth and of its vulnerability. In addressing the Heads of Government at Kuala Lumpur she said: 'Like all the best families, we have our share of eccentricities, of impetuous and wayward youngsters and of family disagreements. But we also have our wise uncles and aunts and the solid, dependable family members on whom everyone relies'.

32 It is this analogy of human relationships which is the strength of the Commonwealth. The Queen has seen Heads of Government come and go but, by her continuing presence at CHOGMs, her Christmas broadcasts and her presence at Commonwealth Games, as well as her tireless visits to member countries, she epitomises such relationships.

33 In its evolution the Commonwealth has benefited from distinct characteristics that equip it to play a particular role on the international stage. That role is to work at the interfaces of the international system,

to build bridges between different political, economic and geographic interests. Ideally it acts as a forum in the search for compromise and consensus in the service of its membership and the international community as a whole.

34 It is in its manner of doing business that the Commonwealth is most different from other international organisations. For all its variety and growth over the years it has managed to retain the virtues of intimacy and informality. The biennial summits of Commonwealth leaders uniquely reflect these qualities which in turn are replicated at other Commonwealth meetings, be they ministerial, official, or unofficial.

Commonwealth Heads of Government Meetings

35 Every other year there is a meeting of the Commonwealth Heads of Government and, judging by the high degree of attendance by Heads of Government, these biennial meetings are of significance and importance to them. Each lasts for about a week and there are three features which are common to all of them. First, the Heads of Government hold a 'retreat'. This takes place away from the formal meeting place and without officials. Secondly, HM the Queen always attends the meeting and immediately prior to it pays a state visit to the host country. Thirdly, during the meeting the Queen takes the opportunity to hold personal discussions with each Head of Government. These discussions are entirely confidential with no other person present and they are greatly valued.

36 At the Kuala Lumpur CHOGM, the meeting at which Pakistan was welcomed back to the Commonwealth, 35 out of the then 49 members of the Commonwealth were represented by their Heads of State, President or Prime Minister. The Secretary-General of the Commonwealth is a full member of the Meeting and it is serviced by staff members of the Commonwealth Secretariat. Many Heads of Government bring Ministers of State and Civil Servants with them, their presence depending on the subjects to be discussed. A number of meetings of sub-committees and special working parties are held alongside the CHOGM meeting.

37 Heads of Government discuss world issues, review Commonwealth affairs, and set the Commonwealth on its course for

the next two years. The biennial summits have no counterparts as a regular assembly of leaders from all continents. Recent venues have included Lusaka (1979), Melbourne (1981), New Delhi (1983), Nassau (1985), Vancouver (1987) and Kuala Lumpur (1989). Similarly meetings of Ministers of, for example, Finance, Health and Agriculture, take place on a regular basis.

38 Political dialogue is at the heart of the association. The visibility and impact of Commonwealth consultations, particularly at the level of Heads of Government, has been transformed as the standing and importance of independent Commonwealth countries within the international community has grown. This in turn has given greater weight to the influence of the Commonwealth as a whole. No other forum provides the same opportunities for leaders of North and South to confront emerging global issues such as the environment, conditions for sustained development, the debt crisis and illicit drug trafficking, free of procedural bureaucratic and linguistic difficulties.

39 The advantage of the use of English as the language of discussion is very considerable. It not only enables formal discussions to proceed without interpretation but, perhaps even more importantly, allows informal discussion to take place in a way which is simply not possible where language barriers exist. A lot of the effort of translating official documents into other languages is avoided.

40 Heads of Government Meetings have developed a character which is unique amongst large international gatherings. Sessions are private, frank and informal, and in both plenaries and many smaller meetings allow for the development of understanding and friendship.

41 The bonds that tie the Commonwealth together are many: history, language, the institutions of government and law, education, social custom and sport. It is an association prompted by the past, but not beholden to it. No grand design has charted its growth, but as it has evolved so it has been deeply involved in the process of decolonisation and development.

42 As an association which reflects the interdependent character of the modern world, non-racialism has to be a basic principle, not just in a merely negative sense but in terms of a positive creative partnership of different races. Active opposition to racism and racial prejudice is not only a necessary consequence of the Commonwealth's

membership: it is also an expression of its deepest beliefs. For this reason South Africa left the Commonwealth in 1961 and Fiji's membership lapsed in 1987.

43 In the Commonwealth's membership is to be found a high proportion of the world's absolute poor (para. 238ff). Heads of Government have sought to obtain agreement that change in international economic structures is necessary, just and ultimately in everyone's interest. In pursuit of this objective, they have set up a series of expert groups, composed of nationals of member countries at different stages of development, to analyse problems, and to propose solutions. Their reports may not have eye-catching titles, but they have contributed to a global dialogue.

44 Such expert group reports on these matters include: *Towards a New International Economic Order* (1975-7); *The Common Fund* (1977); *Co-operation for Accelerating Industrialisation* (1978); *The World Economic Crisis* (1980); *Protectionism: Threat to International Order* (1982); *The North-South Dialogue: Making it Work* (1982). An expert group was set up to consider developing country debt. Its report, *The Debt Crisis and the World Economy*, (1984) described the debt situation as unsustainable and warned that the world's financial safety was balanced on a knife edge.

45 Half the member states of the Commonwealth have populations of less than a million people each, and a quarter less than 200,000. Following discussion of the special problems and needs of these states at the 1979 Lusaka Heads of Government Meeting, the Commonwealth Secretariat has undertaken special programmes of assistance to small member states. Further details are given in *The Commonwealth and the Environment* (Chapter 11).

46 In recent years, small countries have accounted for more than half of the Commonwealth Fund for Technical Co-operation's programme expenditure. Key government officials have been trained, and the Secretariat has given special attention to the interests of small states. It has assisted governments to define their maritime boundaries under the Law of the Sea and has helped them exploit the resources of these maritime zones. It has supported proposals to set up regional legal units, facilitated contacts with countries to keep abreast of international developments, and has also assisted them in export promotion, industrial development and education.

47 The 1985 Commonwealth report, *Vulnerability: Small States in the Global Society*, was an important initiative in alerting the international community to the problems of small states and suggesting measures to improve their economic and political security. Other threats to small states are also receiving attention, such as the effects of climatic change, sea-level rise and flooding. In the wake of the report the Commonwealth-funded office for small states in New York was enlarged and this has enabled even more small states to maintain diplomatic representation at the UN.

The Secretariat

48 The main agency for joint endeavours of the Commonwealth is the Commonwealth Secretariat, established by Heads of Government in 1965. By international standards the Secretariat with a staff of 400 is small. It co-ordinates the work of the association, organises inter-governmental consultations, services Commonwealth meetings and committees. It conducts programmes of co-operation working on an inter-disciplinary basis. It works under the overall direction of Commonwealth governments. At their 1989 Meeting, Heads of Government elected Chief Emeka Anyaoku from Nigeria as Secretary-General, to succeed Shridath Ramphal of Guyana.

49 The Secretariat is active in international, political and economic affairs, many types of co-operation for promoting sustained development, and in such areas as education, health, law, science, youth and the role of women in development. The Secretariat budget for 1990/91 was £7,944,520. Contributions by member governments to the Secretariat budget are on an agreed scale, based on population and national income, with the scale for contributions to the UN used as a broad guide. The main agency for Commonwealth multilateral development work is the Commonwealth Fund for Technical Co-operation (CFTC) which has played a pioneering role in fostering co-operation between developed and developing countries (para. 231).

50 In 1985, a Human Rights Unit was established in the Secretariat's International Affairs Division to assist in promoting understanding and respect for human rights in the Commonwealth. Now in its sixth year, the Unit has been developing its role with a programme of conferences, workshops and seminars and commissioning studies on humanitarian issues, and liaising with relevant international and non-governmental organisations.

Non-Governmental Organisations (NGOs)

51 Important though governmental or 'official' contacts are, they form only a part of the evolution of the modern Commonwealth, and increasingly governments have been using NGOs as a means of dispensing official development aid, believing them to be more effective instruments than governments for this purpose. The network of NGOs has grown rapidly: organisations concerned with aid, development, education and technical training. There is a great variety of non-governmental and unofficial organisations which draw together the people of the Commonwealth through their activities. We name some of the major ones. These are vital to the development of mutual understanding between peoples from diverse backgrounds which is at the core of the Commonwealth.

52 The Commonwealth Parliamentary Association is an organisation of Parliaments, rather than governments, and its members respect all shades of political opinion. The annual conference is therefore a unique opportunity for Parliamentarians, be they Ministers or backbenchers, government or opposition, party representatives or independents, to exchange views on the major political issues of the day and on the systems they use to conduct public business. They are therefore better able to understand the political policies of other nations and the effect of their own policies in the international community, and better able to assess their own parliamentary systems in the light of practices and procedures used elsewhere.

53 The Commonwealth Trust, established in 1988, brings together the Royal Commonwealth Society and the Victoria League for Commonwealth Friendship for the better realisation of the ideals of promoting ideas and understanding, fostering links between peoples and nations and providing an environment for the meeting of minds. The home of the Trust, Commonwealth House in Northumberland Avenue, London, has become a venue for discussion of Commonwealth affairs by statesmen, diplomats, academics and people from all walks of life. The Trust puts a high priority on encouraging Commonwealth youth, sponsoring, for example, regular mock 'Heads of Government Meetings' for students in different countries.

54 An important link between the 'official' and 'unofficial' Commonwealth is the Commonwealth Foundation which has as a

major objective promoting closer co-operation between Commonwealth professionals. The Foundation is funded by member governments. It makes grants for attendance at small conferences and workshops for study visits and training attachments within the Commonwealth; provides financial support to Commonwealth professional associations and professional centres; funds short-term fellowship schemes, in co-operation with other organisations, to promote Commonwealth understanding, mid-career training and the widening of professional experience in fields such as agriculture, planning, health and the media and culture; and makes grants to facilitate the flow of professional information through the distribution of publications.

55 In order to pursue its enlarged mandate from Commonwealth Heads of Government, the Foundation has been promoting better understanding of the work carried out by non-governmental organisations. It has also encouraged the strengthening of information links through facilitating the establishment of NGO Commonwealth liaison units in each Commonwealth country.

56 There are now in the region of 300 Commonwealth non-governmental organisations which embrace, for example, health, industry, international understanding, science, human rights, sport, youth and many other areas. A large number of them have social and informational functions: they help people from different countries meet in friendship and understanding, and help their members learn more about the lives of people in other Commonwealth countries.

Other links

57 Institutions are necessary to the Commonwealth, but the Commonwealth is more than its institutions. As well as the links between governments, and shared traditions in education, law, administration and other fields, there are connections in the arts and in sport. The achievements of writers, actors, film-makers, musicians, dancers, painters, sculptors are their own, but the Commonwealth gains from their several contributions. Many artists find a wide public in other Commonwealth countries, particularly, but by no means exclusively, within their region.

58 Commonwealth literature reflects the bonds of common language and traditions, which are frequently reflected even in writing in

Commonwealth countries in languages other than English. Universities in a number of countries, both within and beyond the Commonwealth, offer courses in Commonwealth literature, and the Association for Commonwealth Language and Literature Studies promotes academic work and contact in this field.

59 The Commonwealth Institute is a cultural and educational agency, set up by Act of Parliament and with all High Commissioners in London on its Governing Body, to promote awareness of the contemporary Commonwealth. Its centre in Kensington runs a continuous programme of events for the general visitor, specialists and school-children, often built round a single theme (e.g. Commonwealth Africa in 1984, the Commonwealth Caribbean in 1986 and the Commonwealth Pacific in 1988). Special attractions include art exhibitions, traditional music and dance and festivities for schools. There are three floors of permanent exhibitions on the Commonwealth countries, an exhibition on 'Africa, history and achievements', and a new permanent exhibition about the Caribbean region, 'Caribbean Eye'. The Education Department co-ordinates a significant outreach programme and the Institute works closely with other Commonwealth and international bodies.

60 The Commonwealth is about development which is centred on people, for it is the citizens of the Commonwealth who are its most important resource.

Chapter 3

BRITAIN IN THE COMMONWEALTH

61 If we are to understand why there exists a degree of hostility in some quarters in Britain towards the Commonwealth as an organisation, and some wider disillusionment as well, it is important to try and see how these have developed.

The nature of Britain: its island status

62 It has been suggested to us that there are probably some deep-rooted matters to explore. Britain has been an island nation for a very long while and we remain instinctively wary about other peoples. There are clearly difficulties for any ex-imperial power in developing mutually satisfactory relationships with its former colonies. British attitudes have been more recently affected by one widespread misconception. Has not Britain joined the European Community (EC)? Did it not thereby 'give up the Commonwealth'? The fact that Britain's membership of the EC is no more at odds with its membership of the Commonwealth than, say, Malaysia's membership of ASEAN (the Association of South East Asian Nations) or Papua New Guinea's of the Pacific Forum, has not been easily grasped.

63 Even so there is arguably a long list of reasons why British disillusionment with the Commonwealth periodically runs deep, and these deserve pondering.

Historical reasons pre-1950

64 The starting point is to recall that up to the period immediately after the Second World War great pride was taken by Britain in the British Commonwealth. Apart from conflicts in Ireland there has been no repetition of the American War of Independence. Against earlier expectations, the original Dominions – Canada, Australia, New Zealand, and South Africa – while developing their own national

characteristics and styles of government, freely chose to remain within the British Commonwealth when they secured international recognition as independent nation states. With the exception during the Second World War of Eire (though not of the Irish as a whole), they all participated extensively on Britain's side in both World Wars (as the older ones had in the Boer War as well). There was much co-operation in defence planning: in the development of the sterling bloc; and in the imperial preference system developed at the Ottawa Conference in 1932.

65 After the Second World War Britain's claims to be one of the world's great powers (despite her largely singlehanded defiance of Nazi Germany in 1940-41) came under threat. In her efforts to remain a great power in a world now dominated by the United States and the Soviet Union, Britain envisaged that the Commonwealth could play a major role in buttressing its position. Despite the decisions of Burma in 1948 and Ireland in 1949 to leave the Commonwealth that ambition seemed to be attaining some success when on their independence in 1947 Pakistan and Ceylon, and more particularly – on becoming a Republic – India in 1949, decided to become members. Thereafter Ghana and Malaya in 1957, Nigeria in 1960 and many others sought to belong as well.

66 But things did not quite work out as much influential British opinion had hoped. 'It was a noble ideal – the Commonwealth', Lord Beloff characteristically remarked in 1972; 'a pity it failed'. In 1949 'the British Commonwealth' had become 'the Commonwealth of Nations' – no longer principally a 'British' institution, now increasingly a multi-racial one. By the 1960s it was no longer dominated by people of British stock. Far from being a buttress against Britain's changing position in the world, it had become a self-created arena in which Britain appeared to be endlessly abused.

67 What had happened? It needs to be remembered that there was always more friction (not least with the white Dominions) behind the scenes than was openly recognised. At the turn of the century the 'white' colonies had opposed all idea of 'Imperial Federation'. Between the two World Wars Hughes the Australian Prime Minister, Mackenzie King the Canadian, Hertzog the South African, and de Valera the Irishman, concerned to pursue their own countries' interests, were at least as large thorns in the side of the British as any

of their African, Asian and other successors. The fault, moreover, was by no means all on one side. There are Australians, for example, who have long called the failure of the British to meet their longstanding promise to hold the Singapore base against the Japanese in 1942 'the Great Betrayal'; New Zealanders bewildered at being abandoned by Britain's entry into the EC; West Indians angered by Britain's handling of their sugar crops.

68 Moreover, in contrast with the French, the British did not provide former tropical colonies with the aid and assistance on a scale that might have welded the Commonwealth as closely to them as some of the former French colonies (Ivory Coast, Senegal etc.) are to France. Of course the British Empire was always larger than the French (and for understandable reasons in particular cases the French only chose to assist some of their former colonies). Yet just when in the late 1940s Britain might have advanced considerable aid to the new South Asian Commonwealth, she was overtaken by the post-Second World War economic crisis and the 1949 devaluation. Later in the 1960s when she might have helped her African ex-colonies substantially she was plunged into her 1960s economic crisis and the 1967 devaluation. France, meanwhile, a founding member of the EC, was much more readily able to provide support to some of its former colonies, and the relationship remained much closer.

69 Britain had other problems too. Whilst there were defence arrangements with the original Dominions, and initially with Pakistan and Ceylon, the attempts to create a defence agreement with India in 1947 never succeeded, and the one with Nigeria in 1960 quickly collapsed. In 1951, because of the memory of Singapore 1942, even the Australians, so long staunch in their attachment to Britain, went to the length of making the ANZUS Treaty between Australia, New Zealand and the United States, from which Britain was excluded. The old notion of collaborative 'Imperial Defence' soon became a thing of the past.

70 From the late 1950s onwards, moreover, Britain moved to check Commonwealth immigration. That engendered a great deal of heat on all sides, and did the Commonwealth connection no good at all.

Major episodes post-1950

a) SUEZ

71 There were then several major episodes which cumulatively did enormous damage to the regard in which the Commonwealth was held in influential circles in Britain. As in Britain itself, there were deep divisions within all of the original Dominions over the Suez affair in 1956. Immediately following Egypt's nationalisation of the Suez Canal, Nehru, India's Prime Minister, urged Nasser to be cautious. Nehru was outraged, however, by Britain's use of force over Suez; but many British Conservatives were no less outraged by Nehru's failure to denounce with corresponding vehemence the simultaneous Soviet repression of the Hungarian uprising. Over Suez the Commonwealth was deeply divided, with the British, the Australian, and the New Zealand governments on the one side, and those of the Asian members and Canada – which thus prevented a split on straight racial lines – on the other (South Africa kept itself to the sidelines). Eden's serious breach of previous Commonwealth practice, by deliberately keeping his Commonwealth partners uninformed of his intentions, only made matters worse.

b) SOUTH AFRICA

72 That was bad enough. The situation was aggravated following the accession of the first African members of the Commonwealth by the dispute over South African membership in 1960-61. The Nationalists had come to power in South Africa in 1948, and by 1960 the worst excesses of their apartheid regime were in full operation. Early in that year the Sharpeville killings occurred. At the same time South Africa began to move towards becoming a Republic. That raised the technical point which followed upon the arrangements made in 1949 when India became a Republic but remained within the Commonwealth, by which continued membership by a country on becoming a Republic required the agreement of its other members. This was ordinarily agreed (e.g. for Ghana in 1960). But in 1960 the new member Malaya, sought to deny this to South Africa, and the issue came to a head in March 1961 when Julius Nyerere announced that if South Africa were to remain in the Commonwealth the about-to-be-independent Tanganyika (later Tanzania) would not join. That led to a major contretemps (in which Canada took the Afro-Asian

side) which resulted in South Africa withdrawing its application to continue its membership. That was very much at odds with the wishes of the Macmillan British Conservative government and fuelled the growing distaste in such circles for the changing Commonwealth.

c) RHODESIA/ZIMBABWE

73 All this was made several times worse by the elongated crisis over Rhodesia. By the time white Rhodesia issued its Unilateral Declaration of Independence in November 1965 the Commonwealth had been substantially enlarged by an influx of new members especially from Africa. From an early date some of them demanded that Britain should use force against the Rhodesian rebellion (as it had against Mau Mau, the Malaysian Communists, EOKA etc.). But Wilson, Britain's Labour Prime Minister, refused to do so; public opinion polls in Britain were showing that only a tiny proportion of British opinion would have supported him if he had. Wilson accordingly had to face a succession of angry Commonwealth meetings – particularly in Lagos in January 1966 and in London in September 1966. At the latter a Zambian minister denounced him as 'a racist', and not unnaturally Wilson lost his temper. Britain thereafter proved powerless to resolve the Rhodesian crisis, and it was only brought to an end in 1979-80 – following the army revolt in Portugal and the ending of the Portuguese African empire in 1974-5; by the mounting success of the Zimbabwean guerrillas within Rhodesia itself; and by Commonwealth pressure on Mrs Thatcher, not least by some 'white' members of the Commonwealth at the time of the Lusaka meeting of Heads of Government in 1979, to call a comprehensive constitutional conference in London. Even though the affair was then satisfactorily settled, there can be no doubt that it generated great irritation in a number of circles in Britain at what was seen to be the intolerable treatment Britain had received from the Commonwealth.

d) THE SANCTIONS DEBATE

74 Nor was there any relief thereafter. For the 1980s then saw the continuing, and frequently bitter, dispute between Mrs Thatcher, Britain's Conservative Government and their supporters on the one side, and every one of the other Commonwealth countries on the other over the issue of sanctions against apartheid in South Africa.

During the course of this dispute Britain became severely isolated (Chapter 9).

Other reasons for a negative response

75 The depth of dismay, disgust indeed, with all of this in many British circles is not too difficult to understand. It was not just, moreover, that this treatment was at the hands of the Commonwealth's Afro-Asian members. Canada had invariably come down on the opposing side against Britain. So had Australia over Zimbabwe and South Africa; and New Zealand was not far behind either.

76 In some respects things were not helped by the creation in 1965 of the Commonwealth Secretariat, with its influential Secretary-General, and by the practice after 1971 (except in the Queen's Silver Jubilee year 1977) of holding Heads of Government Meetings outside London. Hitherto Commonwealth affairs had been masterminded by the British Cabinet Secretary and Britain's Commonwealth Relations Office. Now everything seemed to have slipped from their grasp.

77 Moreover, the situation appeared to many in Britain to be all the worse because so many of its former colonies had fallen into the hands of one party states, authoritarian rulers, and coup-elevated dictators. Whilst in many particular cases this was all too dreadfully true, as an overall picture it was quite palpably exaggerated. Much the greater part of the Commonwealth, not least in most of the Caribbean and the South West Pacific, remained democratic, but that was scarcely mentioned.

78 Thus it was that in much popular British perception *The Commonwealth Experience* (to use the title of one major study) became so highly negative.

Value of membership to other Commonwealth countries

79 The problem here for British opinion of this kind is that in practically every other member country the 'Commonwealth Experience' has by contrast been generally very positive, and the consequence is that, whatever its critics in Britain may desire, the Commonwealth is not about to collapse, go away or disband.

80 We comment elsewhere on the value which Heads of Government very evidently attach to their regular biennial meetings. No doubt many of them welcome these as occasions to be enjoyed. The substance, however, is that these constitute the one occasion when so many Heads of Government (and for many of them the only occasion) can meet their peers – who quite literally speak the same language – and 'test the water' right around the globe. There have by now been numerous cases of Heads of Government who began by being sceptical of the Commonwealth , but soon became enthusiasts for it. Prime Minister Muhathir of Malaysia refused to attend the meetings in 1981 and 1983. He was persuaded, however, to attend in 1985 and 1987, and became so enamoured of what he found that he invited Heads of Government to meet next in Kuala Lumpur in 1989, and there agreed to chair the High Level Appraisal Group to review the Commonwealth's whole future. The expectation was that this would be composed of officials. Heads of Government decided, however, that it should be composed from amongst their own number, Mrs Thatcher included. There could be no greater vote of confidence in the way the Commonwealth had been evolving.

81 Elsewhere we review the Commonwealth's other attractions. But here let us note one further consideration. Just as Britain used the Commonwealth in the 1940s-60s to ease the trauma of the end-of-empire, so many of its other members have learned to use their membership for their own particular purposes too:

Canada has steadily supported the Commonwealth both as a means of expressing its more sympathetic attitude towards the developing world, and as a way of distinguishing itself from its more powerful north American neighbour;

Australia because it allows its leaders to cut a larger figure in the world than they can do anywhere else;

many an African state because it has enabled them to focus global opinion on southern African questions far more effectively than any other institution;

most of its smaller members because only here are they given the hearing they are usually denied elsewhere. (Who else, for example, would have heeded the anguished concern of the Maldive Islands over their likely inundation as a consequence of sea-level rise following upon global warming than the Commonwealth did in 1987-9?)

India, by opposing Pakistan's desire to rejoin the Commonwealth in the period 1979-89 (following its precipitate withdrawal upon Bangladesh's recognition in 1972), used its Commonwealth membership to deprive Pakistan of full international approbation. Following Benazir Bhutto's democratic election in 1989 India was then able to display its magnanimity by leading the way for Pakistan's re-entry to the Commonwealth.

These things are the stuff of international politics.

Its opportunities: examples

82 Since the Commonwealth is not about to disappear it would be well if Britain once again seized the opportunities its Commonwealth connections allow to advance its own interests and recognised the wider advantages of associating with its other members more closely. Instead, for example, of trying to solve the problem of Hong Kong's '1997' refugees on its own (and it is sad that the Foreign and Commonwealth Office did not start the discussion on Hong Kong within the context of the Commonwealth) Britain could still fashion a contingency plan with the considerable number of other Commonwealth countries – Canada, Australia, New Zealand, Singapore for a start – who have long been taking Hong Kong migrants anyway.

83 In this respect 1988-89 saw one encouraging development. Mrs Thatcher visited Australia for its bicentennial celebrations. Whilst there she opened a new dialogue with the Australian government as a consequence of which Britain can draw in a privileged manner (in a way none of her European partners can) on Australian's growing expertise on the Asia/Pacific region – economically the fastest growing region in the world – in exchange for providing Australia with similar privileged access to Britain's expertise on Europe 1992. Over the preceding twelve years no Australian Prime Minister had visited London (other than to pay respects to Australia's Queen, whom she shares with Britain); there seemed little point in doing so. In 1989, however, upon Mrs Thatcher's invitation Prime Minister Hawke came to London with three of his senior ministers to maintain the dialogue, and despite continuing differences over South African sanctions a much healthier relationship began to be established. It would be an excellent model to follow on other Commonwealth fronts.

84 There are two points to add. As the Cold War ends and the superpower struggle ceases to hold centre-stage, regional concerns begin to preoccupy the world more and more: Europe; the Soviet Union; Asia/Pacific; China; the Americas; and now, with a new urgency, the Middle East. But, as the Gulf Crisis has shown, the world continues to shrink fast. 'The West' and Britain comprise an ever decreasing proportion of its total population. This is hardly the time therefore to forgo the well established inter-regional links we already possess – in the Commonwealth particularly. The path of wisdom is to use them, and to let byegones be byegones.

85 It should never be forgotten, moreover, that there are very many more ordinary British people than are generally appreciated who have all manner of personal links with people in other Commonwealth countries which they value and cherish. This is true quite apart from the important Commonwealth immigrant communities in our midst. A good many of these are business and professional people; for many of them the world is a small place already. But there are many others who have relatives, friends, holiday experiences and much else besides which make associations with one or more Commonwealth country a matter of considerable personal importance to them. There is nothing to be said for breaking these bonds, and everything to be said for developing them further.

Chapter 4

THE COMMONWEALTH AS GIFT

86 How are we to judge Britain and the Commonwealth from any value based perspective? Is there any comment that can be made from the world of faith – and of Christian faith in particular?

The moral perspective of institutions

87 It would be convenient to dismiss this type of discussion by the suggestion that institutions are, by their very nature, morally and spiritually neutral. It is individual people and the sum of their attitudes which alone can be commented on in the context of moral and spiritual values. People are good or evil (or a mixture of both); institutions strictly neutral. Institutions, however, reflect the values and objectives of those who create and sustain them. They 'institutionalise' ways of understanding human life in the community. In that respect they either reflect and sustain good and wholesome things or bad and destructive things. Usually they represent a balance of good and not-so-good things and the balance varies from institution to institution.

88 The institutions of 'apartheid' were the product of a deeply distorted ideology carried forward by communities intent on excluding black people from power. One could hardly call the institutions of apartheid 'neutral'. They clearly, from any responsible moral perspective, are part of an evil and destructive order. Similarly, the Nazi state or Stalinist states partake so much of the morally compromised and wicked side of human affairs that they must fall heavily on the evil end of the spectrum of good and evil. By contrast more open and free societies which make some effort at affirming the common humanity and dignity of all members are bound to have features which are good and sustaining for people to live in. It is not that democracies are perfect. It is that, on the whole, they are good for people. They generally help forward the business of peaceful social existence.

The Christian vision of the human and human well-being

89 Judgements of this kind require a moral framework of reference. Religious belief, and Christian belief in particular, provides a basis for the development of such a framework. Faith in God helps in the discovery of what is good and, by implication, what is not good. Thus a vision of the good in human experience is developed and sustained within religious faith. The Christian vision of the human is nourished by the story of Jesus and the experience of Jesus in the continuing life of the Church.

90 A sound moral framework is deeply human. Thus one which arises out of Christian faith will have much in common with all such moral reasoning to be found in human experience born of other faiths or none. The common ground is our human life and our commitment to its well-being. Thus a spectrum of good and evil for use in relation to social and political institutions, developed by Christians, will be attractive well beyond the Christian community.

Affirming what is good in the journey from Empire to Commonwealth

91 What judgement are we to pass on the Commonwealth as an institution and in particular what are we to make of Britain's relationship to it? The first thing that can be said is that the journey of history from which it has emerged is one that needs affirming. The progress illustrated in the last chapter, from Empire through the British Commonwealth to the Commonwealth of Nations tells a story of positive development from dependency on the power of Britain as an Imperial power, through the period of self-determination, towards a mature community of nations seeking to stay together in a voluntary association of mutual interest. That journey is equally wholesome for Britain. From being the power, however well executed, over the affairs of those subject to her power, through adjusting to a role of leading member of a family of independent nations, to being a senior but equal partner in a community of peoples, is a journey which, whilst not always entered into with enthusiasm, has been undertaken to her benefit. We might also suggest that there is some credit in it for all concerned. Not all Empires turn themselves into something else without destroying the historic bonds that have been created in the imperial experience.

92 The bonds of history, have provided the opportunity for exploring ways in which the relationships so created can be turned to mutually beneficial outcomes. All lasting international bodies have a history behind them – events and relationships which brought the parties together. The essence of their continuing viability and success is the capacity to adjust and allow the relationships to change as the circumstances of living change. The fact of the Commonwealth is witness to the possibility that changes can be successfully, if not always painlessly, negotiated. At a time when other major international alliances are going through a period of rapid and traumatic change, the example of the Commonwealth offers hope of success in such journeyings.

93 There are many wholesome features to the Commonwealth. Not the least is that this is an institution whose *raison d'être* is not about defence. This is not a military alliance. Neither is it predominantly an organisation concerned with economic self-interest, although there are crucial and vital economic elements to the workings of the Commonwealth. It is more of a cultural and historic community – bonded together by relationships deep in the heart of each nation's history. Members of the Commonwealth have fought alongside each other in war, which creates a considerable bond – and not least came to the aid of Britain in the great wars of the twentieth century. The Commonwealth is a means of promoting the economic health and prosperity of its members. These, however, are benefits of the relationships rather than their fundamental reason. In a world in which either matters of defence or of economic self-interest are so pressing, it is of particular importance to stress that other sorts of bonds and relationships can form the basis for successful and creative international political bodies.

94 Probing this institution a little deeper we may note other potentially creative aspects of it. It bridges some of the most intractable divisions of our contemporary world. It crosses the major divisions of race. Here is a community of nations – some of which belong to the world of white power and culture and some of which are rooted in black history. Within that are a multiplicity of cultural, religious and ethnic historic experiences. It is worth repeating that the task of confronting and overcoming the powerful and dehumanising forms of racism in our world is a priority task for the Commonwealth. The issue goes to the heart of what the Commonwealth is.

95 Other major divisions are crucially represented in the life of the Commonwealth. The overpowering problems of poverty predominantly to be found in the South are set alongside the problems of wealth predominantly to be found in the North. Both in their own way represent a threat to our fragile environment. Deserts go with poverty and destructive exploitation of the earth's resources with wealth. The Commonwealth is to be found in peoples of Europe and North America and in the peoples of Asia, Africa and the islands. Deeply contrasting experiences, which relate to each other but which might be kept apart from each other, are joined in the Commonwealth. Thus another priority agenda for an agency such as the Commonwealth is the probing of these relationships, the exploration of new ways forward in enabling a better stewardship and sharing of the resources of the earth and a journey of seeking to use power for the benefit of widening sections of this human family. And the recognition that the rich may have rather more to learn from the poor in terms of spiritual values than the poor from the rich.

96 Since the Commonwealth crosses so many divisions and distinctions of culture and expectation, it can be a forum for creative exchange about other matters that cause pain in human experience today. The changing role of women in the world and the implicit changes expected of men as a result is one such matter. Here the mutual engagement of contrasting religious and cultural histories has the potential for making the Commonwealth something good for the life and experience of women in our world. Especially is this so when it is remembered that women bear a large part of the burden of poverty and suffer, often unheard, the abuses of racist cultures. What happens to women might prove to be a lesson which helps us focus the wholesomeness or otherwise of the life of institutions such as the Commonwealth. We spell this out further in Chapter 7.

The Commonwealth's limitations

97 None of this requires us to lose out on a sense of proportion. Idolising the Commonwealth is not a profitable exercise. There are strict boundaries about it which need to be acknowledged and accepted. In one sense it is quite a modest organisation. It does not include the great powers of the contemporary world. The USA are well outside of it. Only Britain links it to the EC, and the history of

Britain's entry to the EC caused some pain to the Commonwealth. China is beyond its boundaries. The implications of this for Hong Kong beyond 1997 are not yet fully clear. The majority of the major oil producing nations of our world are not in it. The powerful Islamic cultures of the Middle East are outside the Commonwealth – although it is worth noting that two-thirds of the world's Islamic population is inside it. The Commonwealth's essential meaning and life is not about the gaining of power. It is a community of nations, linked by history, who have chosen to remain in association. Exaggerated claims and expectations could undermine its effectiveness in those things that can reasonably be expected of it.

98 Much of this, then, indicates that the Commonwealth is a modest international agency, which by its history and character has the capacity to stand for some good and wholesome values in the contemporary world. In the journey of its development from Empire to Commonwealth, its crossing of intractable and destructive divisions and the rich variety of its life and culture it offers the possibility of good rather than evil experience.

Britain and its relationship to the Commonwealth

99 When we focus the discussions about the Commonwealth on to Britain's relationship with it, we are bound to judge its capacity for good or evil against the broader canvas already sketched out. Britain is, in one crucial sense, distinguished from the rest of the Commonwealth. The relationships of all the other members are born out of an imperial past. Britain was the imperial power, the member states former colonies. There are two contrasting ways of understanding this. On the one extreme is the perception that Britain was an oppressive imperial power and that, as her power declined, she preserved her self-interest by seeking a change in the character of the relationship. Empire turned to Commonwealth as a way of adjustment necessary to the British self-interest in the world. On the other end is the perception that Britain as a benevolent power has had to adjust from playing the dominant role of the paternal power in relation to the colonies to learning to share as an equal partner in a community of independent adult nations. No doubt the truth has elements of both within it. Britain has played an oppressive role over its empire and it has had to use its political wit to adjust as this power

declined in the twentieth century. Yet few would doubt but that Britain's influence in the past, albeit dominant and without the free consent of the peoples concerned, had many beneficial effects. One of the reasons for the persistence of the Commonwealth is that the experience of the past, often painful, was not all bad news. Whatever the balance to be struck, however, it is beyond dispute that Britain has had to make major adjustments of attitude and value to move from the world of Empire to that of the world of the Commonwealth.

100 Herein lies the difficulty. For the Commonwealth to be good news in relation to Britain's performance within it, it does require Britain to live by the new situation of the Commonwealth and not lapse into old and outmoded attitude of Empire. Critical issues put this to the test.

Sanctions

101 The first of these concerns process. How does Britain see itself in relation to the other members? Is she ready to collaborate and to allow her own view to be included and adopted in the setting of common debate on the crucial issues? Consider the example of how Britain has approached the question of sanctions against South Africa in the Commonwealth context. The 1989 Commonwealth conference ended up with the public reporting of Britain's distancing from the rest of the Commonwealth over sanctions. The then Prime Minister, Mrs Thatcher, is reported as having been ready to stick to the position of being one over and against all the others. That, of course, is the history. Britain has been over and against all the rest in the origins and nature of the Commonwealth. When Britain was the imperial power, and everyone else part of the imperial realm, it was Britain versus the rest. Thus deep in the culture of this relationship is a history of paternalism and dependency. 'Mummy knows best'. The Commonwealth arose out of the desire to turn this relationship towards a more creative and equal partnership. Old attitudes are deep and die hard and need to be both challenged and adjusted.

102 Adult relationships are bound to encompass differences of view. It is in the management of this that the fundamental attitudes towards the relationships are tested out. The members have to recognise that a body of the nature of the Commonwealth is bound to have divergent interests and needs. That, however, only provides the focus for the

hard work of enabling such a community to find common purposes and shared values. The tendency of Britain, in these international settings, to want to go its own way and assert the predominant rightness of its own view is one that can hinder the possibility of mutual learning and growth of understanding. In the EC Britain has, by the nature of the power of some of the other partners, to yield ground and learn that policy is formed by the interplay of the views of all. A greater readiness to see the value of that process and a disciplined refusal to use its power over and against the Commonwealth to prevent the finding of a way of collaboration – even on such sensitive matters as the sanctions issues – undermines the sense of commitment to Commonwealth. It gives the impression that Britain still wants to play a dominant role which she ought to have left behind a long time ago.

Racism and immigration

103 The sanctions issue is particularly sensitive because of its racist associations. Sanctions are a political weapon aimed at undermining apartheid in South Africa. Racism is an evil which the Commonwealth's very existence opposes. Because Britain has come from a long history of Empire and of the use of its power to promote the slave trade, it has deep historic associations with the roots of contemporary racism. The adjustments from Empire to Commonwealth have certainly not been without difficulty in this area. The painful history of Britain's immigration policy is one in which it is clear that the British people were happy to be in relation to its subordinate people across the world, but much less happy to welcome them into the British community when they chose to take up their rights and settle in this country. The story of immigration policy is one of the steady tightening of the rules to make it first difficult and then virtually impossible for people from the new Commonwealth (predominantly black people) to settle in this country and for their relatives to visit them. The ambivalent attitudes of white culture to black peoples have been close to the surface throughout this history (Chapter 8). Again, there seems to have been doubt as to whether Britain, in its conscience, is willing to leave behind the outlook of Empire and embrace the values of Commonwealth. Britain's refusal to share in the common life of the Commonwealth over sanctions (para. 207ff) raises the shadow of her attitude to the history of racism.

There is therefore a particularly strong moral claim on Britain being seen to share with its partners in the hard road of struggle against apartheid – to be known as having common cause with the black nations of the Commonwealth in exorcising this powerful and evil ghost from the experience of Southern Africa.

Poverty

104 The final matter concerning this relation of North to South is the fight against the crippling reality of poverty (Chapter 10). The causes of poverty are complex but certainly include:

- immense debt burdens, which mean that for many parts of the world the net flow of resources is from impoverished to rich countries;
- adverse terms of trade which sweep away hard-won progress as commodity prices fall;
- the need for land reform: how can food production and well-being be maximised if people do not have a stake in the land?
- past ill-conceived development policies;
- the population explosion;
- natural and man-made disasters and conflict.

It is therefore far too simple just to lay the causes of poverty at the door of the abuse of power by wealthy nations and institutions. It is true that the functioning of the international economic order and its institutions is not always helpful to enabling poverty stricken nations to escape from the awfulness of mass poverty. It is also true that oppression, injustice, the abuse of power and civil strife leave the poor in deeper distress and that some of these features have been endemic to some of the newer nations of our modern world.

105 Economic procedures and policies must be sustainable. Careful balances have to be struck between the obvious and manifest interest of the poorest nations of the South and the self-interest of the North. The danger is that the Northern nations think first and fundamentally about their own interests when pursuing aid and development policies towards the South. Conditions can be attached which have little to do with the needs of the weaker partner and much to do with the economic continuance of the powerful. The Commonwealth offers Britain a unique opportunity to pursue a value-based and principled

course designed to promote the well-being of the South. It can do it by a number of means. It can use the unique relationships of the Commonwealth to engage continually with the experiences of the poor. Thus the challenge of poverty is always before us because we are in a community of which they are a crucial part. The Commonwealth could enable nations such as Britain to become a Northern voice in the international community seeking the welfare of the poorer nations. That leads on to suggesting that this unique relationship offers Britain an opportunity to press the case of the poor within the other communities of power of which she is a part – the EC and the special relationships with the USA. Whilst Britain's route into this is from the Commonwealth, the outcome is about more than the Commonwealth because the needs of struggling nations across the world are included by the ever-widening circles of international relationships.

106 The capacity of Britain therefore to collaborate with her Commonwealth partners, to share the struggle to roll back the history of racism and to play a role in bridging the needs of the South into the life of the North become a moral test of the value of the Commonwealth when seen from the perspective of Britain's membership of it. Stated positively, they provide the agenda for Britain to share in enabling the Commonwealth to fulfil its potential as an agency for human flourishing in the world.

The Commonwealth as 'gift'

107 Is it possible to make a comment of a theological character out of all of this? This is not the place to offer a substantial theological rationale. (See Chapter 13.) One particular note is worth striking at this point. We have noted that institutions partake either of good or of evil – or more usually a mixture of both. We must judge both what they are in themselves and the use made of them by their members. We have seen that the Commonwealth is a distinctive sort of international body. Its primary concerns are neither related to defence nor to purely economic self-interest. It is a body which has emerged out of a history of empire. Out of what was, by its very nature, a difficult and problematic way of establishing ties across the world, has arisen a body whose members cross many of the difficult divisions of our world. There is so much to commend it. Indeed we might see it as a *gift* to the world of international affairs standing for the possibility of quality relationships which as a benefit – not a *raison d'être* – serve the

interests of its partners. Things which partake of the nature of gift fit well with the Christian pattern of human life in relation to God. We find God comes to us in the gifts he offers for our flourishing as people created in his image and for the enjoyment of his love. This is focused in the gift God brings to human life in Jesus who creates, restores, heals and nurtures our humanity. All experiences of the human community which, in some significant measure partake of this pattern, should be cherished for as long as they serve these good ends.

Britain's need to adjust to the Commonwealth: The Church of England's need to adjust to the Anglican Communion

108 This is not to suggest that the Commonwealth is either perfect or indestructible. Its future is entirely dependent on its members continuing to understand its character and to be ready to evolve with its changing purposes. Here lies the challenge to Britain. The Commonwealth, we say, is a good thing and offers the possibility of good things to its members and, indeed to the wider international community. None of this will add up to much if Britain, which has had such a particular role in its emergence, finds it is troublesome to adjust to the very institution it has so successfully helped to create. We have to play the role of a member with the necessary disciplines of corporate life. The temptations to want to play the role of pivotal power and the counterbalancing temptation to others to collude with Britain in this must be resisted. Such attitudes belong to a set of relationships that have long since ceased to be appropriate. If carried forward today they would have a corrupting and destructive effect. That surely, from a moral and spiritual perspective, would be something bad and unworthy. It is a parallel temptation to that of the Church of England wanting to be determinative of the shape of Anglicanism in the world today. The nature of Anglicanism has to be understood from the shared life of the whole Anglican community. Similarly the meaning of our continual participation in the Commonwealth, with all the depth of history of British involvement, has to be shaped by the life of the whole body. For Britain, now a multicultural society living in a mobile world, that is full of potential for good. It would be a tragedy if either Britain or the other members of the Commonwealth lost out on its potential because we all forgot the nature of the journey that has been travelled.

Chapter 5

THE ANGLICAN COMMUNION

109 Our terms of reference call for a perspective from the Church of England's membership of the Anglican Communion on what Britain's membership of the Commonwealth entails. Appropriate as this may be in a Church of England report, it should not be taken to imply disregard for other Christian traditions found within the Commonwealth which in many parts of it are stronger than Anglicanism. We are not suggesting that Anglicanism is more significant in the life of the Commonwealth than other Christian denominations, or overlooking the importance of ecumenical co-operation. Rather a parallel is being drawn between a particular piece of ecclesiastical organisation and a particular political association, both of which have their origin in the history of British people in the wider world.

Clarification

110 The comparison is complicated by its being between the Commonwealth membership of, to be precise, the United Kingdom of Great Britain and Northern Ireland on the one hand and, on the other, Anglican Communion membership on the part of one, albeit established, church among those found in one of the four nations that make up the United Kingdom. There is no implied notion that the Church of England is, as it were, the United Kingdom at prayer. Within the confines of Anglicanism, the Church of Wales, the Church of Ireland and the Scottish Episcopal Church have shared historically to a great extent in the Church of England's relation to the church outside these islands, and yet share some of the feelings found in Anglican churches overseas towards the Church of England.

111 The purpose of the comparison is to shed light on our consideration of the Commonwealth and of Britain's role in it. There are obvious differences in both style and substance between a relationship of ecclesial communion and one of political association,

but people with experience of both the Anglican Communion and the Commonwealth tend to find a similarity between the two organisations. Both have arisen out of British expansion into other parts of the world, both are based on a kind of pragmatic co-operation (which may be characteristically British) between autonomous bodies with minimal theorising about principles and no organisational control of members. Thus there is similarity between the ethos of the two organisations, each of which describes itself as a family. The Chicago-Lambeth quadrilateral which serves as a theological basis for the Anglican Communion resembles Commonwealth principles, such as partnership, equality and multi-racialism, in affirming what members share with others outside the organisation rather than anything that differentiates them from the rest.

112 It would no doubt be instructive but considerably more difficult to make a comparison between the Commonwealth and the Baptist World Alliance, the World Methodist Council, the World Alliance of Reformed Churches (of which the Church of Scotland is a member) or the Roman Catholic Church. Drawing parallels with the Anglican Communion is relatively easy.

Historical parallels

113 It is obvious that in many parts of the world the extension of the Anglican Church in the nineteenth and early twentieth centuries was associated with the expansion of British influence as well as of British rule. To say that the gospel followed the flag is to overlook the cases, such as Nigeria and Uganda, where missionaries (often along with traders) preceded any sort of political colonisers, but it is generally true that the church really grew and flourished once some kind of British administration was established.

114 There was then a natural affinity between the political and ecclesiastical institutions set up by British people. Anglican mission stations were naturally run, like the civil administration, in British ways. The same affinity could be seen between the British colonial government and the Presbyterian mission which was prominent in Nyasaland, or the Methodist mission in Fiji. Similar things could be said of Belgian or Portuguese colonies and the Roman Catholic missions in them. A particularly strong form of the relationship between Anglicanism and British administration is shown in the

location on British territory overseas, such as Gibraltar or the Falklands, of Anglican bishoprics ministering to people in foreign countries, on the continent of Europe and in Southern America respectively.

115 As with colonisation so with de-colonisation: the formation of autonomous Anglican Provinces overseas went with the achievement of political independence. The process began in North America where the British government's reluctance to grant repeated requests for an American bishopric led to the consecration of Samuel Seabury in Scotland in 1784, just after United States independence had been won. In working out how to remain in communion with the Church of England while no longer under British rule, the American Church was, effectively, inventing the Anglican Communion. At that time the only autonomous Anglican Church, in addition to the Church of England, was the Scottish Episcopal Church. The nineteenth century saw the formation of other autonomous Anglican Provinces in several parts of the British Empire, and then in the 1950s Archbishop Fisher initiated the establishment of further provinces in Africa. Bishop John Howe comments:

> It is true that by that time the majority of the countries involved were moving towards political independence, but it will not do to limit Archbishop Fisher's accomplishment to a following of the political trend. The new Anglican Provinces of his time came before political independence.

Organisational parallels

116 By such similar processes the Anglican Communion and the Commonwealth have both evolved as free associations of autonomous bodies. As with the independent members of the Commonwealth, so in the Communion

> Each Province has its own Constitution which no other Province can interfere with.

As Commonwealth countries have their parliaments, Anglican Provinces have their Synods, and it is also possible to trace other organisational parallels. Of the Lambeth Conference, the Anglican Consultative Council and the Primates' Meeting, perhaps it is the Primates' Meeting (as was noted in Chapter 1) that most closely resembles the Commonwealth Heads of Government Meeting, the others being comparable with various meetings of Commonwealth ministers and officials. Anglican Communion networks dealing with subjects like family, peace and justice, and refugees, can be compared with Commonwealth associations and the two organisations' secretariats have comparable functions. In both cases the secretariats serve the purposes of consultation and co-operation rather than administering any kind of central authority.

117 There is a partial parallel between the role of HM the Queen as Head of the Commonwealth of independent nations, and that of the Archbishop of Canterbury in the Anglican Communion. The affection in which the Queen is held as symbolic Head of the Commonwealth family is to some extent reflected in the feeling of Anglicans round the world towards the Archbishop of Canterbury who, at the Lambeth Conference in 1988, spoke of trying to be 'a personal and visible presence of the whole Anglican family' on his visits to particular Provinces. Whereas the Queen is Head of State in some 17 Commonwealth countries, the Archbishop of Canterbury is the Primate only of All England, but each acts as a focus of unity embracing a considerable number of countries or churches without necessarily having formal authority over all of them. Another parallel may be found between extra-provincial dioceses under the Archbishop's metropolitical jurisdiction and the Commonwealth's Associated States and Dependencies. Dioceses in this category, which are not at present part of any Province, include those in Korea, Malaysia and Singapore where Provinces are in the process of formation, as well as those in Portugal, Spain and Sri Lanka. Bermuda both falls into the category of Commonwealth Associated States and Dependencies and is also an extra-provincial Anglican diocese under the jurisdiction of Canterbury. The Falkland Islands are to be found in both categories for as long as the church there, which has been part of the Diocese of Argentina, remains in the Archbishop of Canterbury's direct care.

The British style

118 Bishop Howe, with experience of all the Provincial synods, reflects:

> Not only does the style in which a synod works differ from one part of the world to another, but interestingly, the style is often inclined to imitate facets of the political ordering of the country.

But throughout the Anglican Communion and the Commonwealth, a British way of doing things is perceptible. The prevalent use of the English language, and English terminology, has a significant impact on the way things are done and may be a subtle means of continued British dominance. In the case of the Anglican Communion, the continued use in some places of the Book of Common Prayer or Hymns Ancient and Modern is an example of this, which has parallels in civil ceremonies. While each member has its own characteristics, they all show a family likeness that in both organisations inevitably has to do with a certain Britishness. Bishop Howe speaks of 'the transition from what we have described as head office and branch offices to being a world-wide family' and goes on:

> A family holds together largely through affection. This affection, which following gospel terminology is suitably called Christian love, is a powerful bond throughout the Anglican family. Also people travel much more and meet. The importance of having a common objective, and often common problems, tends slowly to develop common ground where before it was less apparent. One importance of affection is that when people meet they like one another.

Membership of larger bodies

119 A further parallel exists between each Commonwealth country's membership of the United Nations and each Anglican Province's membership of the World Council of Churches. There is always the possibility, in both cases, that the existence of the smaller grouping may inhibit the effectiveness of the larger one. There is some anxiety about the effect on the ecumenical movement of what are known as world communions, of which the Anglican is one of the most widespread and cohesive. But a more positive approach is to value the cohesiveness that common history and traditions can give to a smaller grouping. These enable it to develop closer understanding and co-operation, particularly among smaller members, than is possible in the larger, more diffuse body to which the smaller can thereby make a constructive contribution. But in taking this view it is necessary constantly to guard against a tendency towards the exclusiveness of a club for the like-minded.

120 Anglicanism involves consciousness of a vocation to serve a wider purpose. As the then Archbishop of Canterbury, Lord Runcie put it at Lambeth 1988:

> We must never make the survival of the Anglican Communion an end in itself. The churches of the Anglican Communion have never claimed to be

> more than a part of the one Holy Catholic and Apostolic Church. Anglicanism has a radically provisional character which we must never allow to be obscured.

We return to this theme in our final chapter. In a comparable way the relative intimacy of interaction between Commonwealth nations enables them together to be more effective participants in other forms of international co-operation, particularly the United Nations whose purposes are served by Commonwealth principles. In his *Introduction to the Report of the Commonwealth* Secretary-General in 1989, Shridath Ramphal spoke of the Commonwealth as 'an element of togetherness across the world's variety that is good for global polity' and 'helps to make the world a better place'.

121 The last similarity to be noted is that, with all the characteristics already mentioned, each organisation, spanning the deep divisions between rich and poor in the world, contains a majority of African, Asian, American, Caribbean and Pacific people, more so in the Commonwealth than in the Anglican Communion. The combined population of Australia, Britain, Canada and New Zealand accounts for about a tenth of the total population of the Commonwealth. Figures for the Anglican Communion are more difficult to obtain, but on the basis of those collected for the Lambeth Conference in 1978, it seems that, of the 33 million Anglicans outside England, perhaps 14 million were white. The inclusion of a figure of 30 million for the Church of England changes the proportions greatly, but only a fraction of that number are as active as Anglicans tend to be elsewhere. There are probably more Anglicans in church on Sunday in Nigeria than in Britain and the United States combined. And it is among black people that the Anglican Communion is growing while it declines numerically among whites.

Distinctions and differences: not co-terminous

122 After pointing out similarities and parallels between the Anglican Communion and the Commonwealth it is necessary to note important differences between them. The first is that they are not co-terminous although there is substantial overlap between them. The Anglican Communion membership is estimated at under 70 million members in 28 Provinces. Of the 551 Anglican dioceses listed at the 1988 Lambeth Conference, some 244 are in the Commonwealth and

307 outside it. In addition there are 53 dioceses of the United Churches of Bangladesh, Pakistan, North India and South India now in the Commonwealth. Some of the non-Commonwealth dioceses were in countries such as Korea or Peru which were always outside British control, others in countries such as Mozambique or Madagascar which were part of other European empires, others again in countries formerly under British control or members of the Commonwealth, but which are so no longer. The largest group, the Episcopal Church of the USA, has had its own spheres of influence among Anglicans in Latin America and East Asia.

123 Although almost every Commonwealth country has some Anglicans or members of a church in full communion they are very unevenly spread through the Commonwealth. Whereas Anglicans form nearly half the population of Uganda, in a Muslim country like Pakistan members of the United Church are less than one per cent of the population. Overall there is a major quantitative difference: the Commonwealth includes nearly a quarter of the world's population which David Barrett in his *Annual Statistical table on Global Mission: 1990* reckons to number a little under 5,300 million. Of this total, the number of Christians in the world is estimated to be about a third, i.e. just under 1,760 million. The number of Anglicans in the world is given as just under 54 million, which is a little over three per cent of the number of Christians.

124 The last difference to be observed is in the part the English language plays in the two organisations. Whereas (para. 39) Commonwealth meetings use only English, interpreters are needed at the Lambeth Conference, and, to a lesser extent at ACC and Primates' Meetings, for those who work in French, Portuguese, Spanish, Swahili and Japanese. At the same time, by including the American Church, the Anglican Communion encompasses the bond between the Commonwealth and the rest of the English-speaking world.

Issues: learning to adapt to a different role

125 A fundamental question about the Church of England and the Anglican Communion parallels one about Britain and the Commonwealth. Can a nation or church which has been the progenitor of others cope with ordinary membership of the organisation which has evolved to hold them all together? In the

family analogy, the mother country and the mother church are having to consider how to join in family life alongside the children. The dilemma is focused in the question, sometimes wryly asked by Anglicans overseas, whether the Church of England will join the Anglican Communion. Clearly it is difficult for the Church of England, as it is for Britain, to settle for being one member among many in a world organisation whose centre of gravity is elsewhere in many respects, even if its office is in London, and where attitudes and opinions other than British may prevail. According to Bishop Howe, while the Anglican Communion

> sees itself as part of Christ's universal Church, it sees itself also as that part which, in the course of history, was funnelled through Britain – a fact which it sees as interesting but not fundamental.

126 We saw in the last chapter how in recent years the issue of sanctions against the Nationalist government of South Africa has divided the Commonwealth, and Britain has at times been alone against all the other members, illustrating in a dramatic way the question about the nature of Britain's membership (para. 74). However this has not prevented the other members from working together on the issue. In the Anglican Communion, on the other hand, there has been agreement on this issue among the member churches including both the Church of England and the Church of the Province of Southern Africa.

127 But at the same time the Anglican Communion has been divided over the ordination of women, and the treatment of this issue by the Church of England has sometimes given the impression that, and been regarded by other denominations as though, decisions taken elsewhere in the Anglican Communion were of little consequence. It has seemed to some that, until the Church of England decides, the question about women as Anglican priests or bishops is not answered. Although the Church of England has not been isolated on this issue, as Britain has been on the sanctions issue, it illustrates the issue about the manner of each's membership of the Communion or the Commonwealth as well as raising broader questions about the handling of divisive issues in the two organisations.

The Anglican Communion as gift

128 These may be the main points at which consideration of the

Church of England in the Anglican Communion can illuminate thinking about Britain in the Commonwealth. We have seen more than once how both organisations think of themselves as families. We have also (para. 107) spoken of the perception of the Commonwealth as 'gift'. The Pastoral Letter from the 1988 Lambeth Conference entitled *The Family as a Gift from God* is mainly about marriage and children but it also applies the family idea to local congregations, and this can surely be extended to suggest that the worldwide Communion is a gift from God. Here is a possible key to using the inheritance of the past in a way that is creative for the future. Rather than seeing the Anglican Communion as an awkward encumbrance, as some do, many people in the Church of England have found it a gift to save us from an introverted and self-important pre-occupation with our own affairs. It is like parents, worn down by caring for adolescent children, being refreshed by re-discovering them as wise and sensitive adults in a new relationship of mutual caring and sharing. People can be liberated from the burden of others' dependency by the gift of a fresh way of relating to them. Such personal liberation may come in a variety of ways, but the givenness of family life makes it a gift of special immediacy and potential effectiveness. Intimacy and affection may be able to change attitudes where argument and exhortation cannot. What can be true of a natural family may also be applied to an ecclesial family held together by 'bonds of affection', and perhaps also to a family of nations.

The pain implicit in change and development

129 But human change and development do not occur without pain, as the issues of South Africa and the ordination of women show in the evolutionary processes going on in the Commonwealth and the Anglican Communion. The former issue may be in process of resolution, but the latter seems likely to continue to cause pain for a long time whichever decisions are taken in particular Provinces. Recognising suffering as evil, Christians are called to use and transform it. In her contribution to the 1988 Lambeth Conference Elizabeth Templeton suggested a way of doing this by seeing the issue of women's ordination:

> as a gift calling us all to earthed exploration of what Christ and culture mean for each other, how a human church bears God to people, how sacrament and sexuality relate. For these are questions which reach into a

wider world, where on the whole people couldn't care less about the ordination of anyone to anything, because they are too busy living and dying.

130 The suggestion is that where people have a strong sense of mutual commitment and belonging together it may be possible to work at a divisive and painful issue in such a way as to serve a larger purpose. The Eames Commission expressed the hope that:

> the spirit of 'respect' and 'courtesy' spoken of by the Lambeth Conference in connection with differences over women in the episcopate may continue to influence this debate in the Anglican Communion. When differences of principle and practice result in tension, debate, and pain, such a spirit will create a profound unity and communion beyond that which the world knows. If those who find the *exclusion* of women from the priesthood and the episcopate contrary to an understanding of God's justice and the meaning of the Incarnation, and those who find their *inclusion* an unacceptable development of the apostolic ministry, can come together to share each other's burdens and sufferings, then the Anglican Communion will have learned something of the meaning of communion with the God who suffers. And we shall have something to say about the unity of Christians and the unity of all humankind.

131 The issue of women's ordination has led Anglicans to speak of 'impaired communion', that is to say some diminution in the intense togetherness which the idea of communion conveys. In aspiring to bind people together in such a way, a church goes beyond what would normally be sought in a political association. However what can be learned about the use of divisive issues in the church may be applicable to the Commonwealth. Here the divisive issue mentioned has been sanctions against *apartheid* South Africa, the most recent manifestation of the problem of South Africa's falling short of the democratic ideals that the Commonwealth espouses, which led to her withdrawal 30 years ago. The problem does occur in relation to other Commonwealth countries where democratic processes are not in place. Perhaps Anglicans' handling of 'impaired communion' can shed light on, and be illuminated by, the Commonwealth's dealing with the issue of democracy, for example in the provision made by the Heads of Government in Kuala Lumpur in 1989 for monitoring elections in member countries. Interestingly it was Malaysia's own elections which were the first to be monitored in 1990.

Interdependence and autonomy: the church as a sign of unity

132 One of the similarities already touched on between the Anglican Communion and the Commonwealth is their seeking to build voluntary interdependence between autonomous bodies. More complex and less efficient than a system of central control, this pattern which inevitably offers a high degree of mutual vulnerability can perhaps be recognised as a Christian contribution to the human search for acceptable forms of organisation. Without central control, which is hardly an option for the world as a whole, voluntary interdependence of some kind may be the only way of balancing liberty and law and order, and perhaps in the end it has to be rooted in affection. In its concern to be a sign of unity to the world, the church would say so.

133 The 'radically provisional character' of Anglicanism shows its vocation to serve a purpose wider than itself in terms of the unity of the church which in turn serves the wider purpose of its members' being, in Lord Runcie's words, 'instruments of unity and communion to a divided world'. The Anglican Communion does not always live up to this vocation, but that need not preclude commending to the Commonwealth a vocation to serve purposes wider than itself, the achievement of which might render its own existence superfluous.

134 In such a way both Commonwealth and Communion can be seen, each in its own way, as gifts to serve God's purposes for humanity. And while the Church of England learns to use the Anglican Communion as God's gift to save it from its besetting sins, so British people may use the Commonwealth to enable the United Kingdom to play a full part in building the peace and justice of God's kingdom.

PART II

Chapter 6

EDUCATION

Introduction

135 The persistence of the Commonwealth in the face of so many forces that would normally lead to disintegration can be accounted for by reference to the existence of a range of factors which include a common historical experience, the silken threads of sentiment, and a shared framework of understanding, language, law and institutions. Without these ties there would be little to hold together the diverse peoples of the Commonwealth, living at great distances from one another. Education, in its most general sense, and the cultural traditions in which it is rooted, has been one of the key-stones of the Commonwealth.

136 Through the medium of education, ideas first fashioned in Britain were exported overseas, where they played a significant part in the spread of British influence throughout the world, and later played a part in its power being challenged. Many Commonwealth nation-builders were the product of a combination of British education and their own cultural heritage. Those who studied in Britain include Gandhi, Nehru, Jinnah, Abdul Rahman, Nkrumah, Nyerere, Kenyatta, Banda, Williams and Manley – to name but a few.

137 It must be recognised that the export of British education to the far-flung reaches of the Empire was not always an unalloyed good. Many people grew up confronting a view that their culture was in some sense 'second-rate', with all the world's wisdom residing with the British. In addition, various negative sterotypes that reflected racist or sexist attitudes were to be found in the content and process of colonial education. However, it has been a singular achievement of the Commonwealth that its policies on education have generally worked to restore a sense of equal respect between its various peoples.

Commonwealth Ministers of Education Meetings

138 Commonwealth Ministers of Education have been meeting regularly to discuss issues of common interest and to review co-operation since 1959. The principles which they then articulated remain equally relevant today:

> Education they stressed, is fundamental to the strength and stability of the Commonwealth, and to social justice and human dignity which must be its inspiration.

Since then, Commonwealth Education Ministers have reaffirmed this principle when considering a number of practical measures designed to facilitate its implementation. In recent times, they have focused in particular on overcoming difficulties that have arisen from decisions by a number of the more developed countries, notably Britain and Australia, to levy fees on overseas students. Such decisions highlight the problems of reconciling a narrow view of self-interest with the advantages of a more open policy.

139 As an example of the range of concerns of the Ministers, they endorsed at their 1987 meeting in Nairobi six major themes as guidelines for the Education Work Programme of the Commonwealth Secretariat. These were:

- school to work transition and vocationally oriented education;
- distance learning and the Commonwealth of Learning;
- Commonwealth student mobility and higher education;
- education development in the small states of the Commonwealth;
- personnel information records and management in education systems;
- science, technology and mathematics education.

Educational developments in the Empire

140 In a significant number of cases the extension of Western (and predominantly British) forms of education to those people who now make up the Commonwealth was instituted by Christian missionaries in the nineteenth century. Throughout the Empire there was, however, a gradual but increasing role for British administrators in the control of education. Arguments between 'Orientalists' and 'Anglicists' over the content and form of education were finally

resolved in India in favour of the 'Anglicist' cause with the publication of Macaulay's *Education Minute* in 1834, which established the principle that

> ...the great object of the British Government ought to be the promotion of European literature and science among the natives of India.

141 Something of this paternalistic attitude lived on into the twentieth century. Despite having experienced the uncomfortable outcomes of their policies in India, the British persisted in the belief that only a liberal western education would improve the condition of 'native peoples'. However, partly as a result of work done by bodies such as the Phelps-Stokes Fund in the 1920s, this attitude was balanced in Africa by support for the maintenance of African languages, the use of African men and women as teachers, and the education of women and girls. Subsequent developments in the 1930s saw education also being seen as needing to be vocationally oriented, with a view to improving standards of health and agricultural production in the less-developed colonies.

Commonwealth links in education

142 Commonwealth-wide initiatives in general education have a long history. In 1901 the Legion of the Empire was established to 'encourage education co-operation between Britain and the Empire'. That objective was subsequently forwarded by the work of official bodies such as the Visual Instruction Committee of the Colonial Office which sought to preserve cohesion in the Empire by encouraging the wide diffusion of knowledge of its 'geography, history, resources, climate and races'. In many respects the Commonwealth Institute took on some of these functions after its reorganisation in 1958.

143 Although bodies such as the Cambridge Local Examinations Syndicate continue to provide a sensitive but pervasive link between Britain and other members of the Commonwealth, to a large degree the systems of primary and secondary education in each of the member nations are now autonomous.

144 Of key importance to the maintenance of educational links in the Commonwealth is the network of associations that exists between universities. When Britain helped establish institutions of higher

education beyond its borders, those responsible for planning this endeavour could draw upon several models. The selection of an appropriate archetype depended upon a number of factors including the demands, experiences and expectations of local people, the existing educational base and the backgrounds and preferences of officials and founding academics. With the exception perhaps of some of the older Canadian foundations, the influence of Oxford and Cambridge was fairly slender. The quality of their scholarship has helped, however, to set what Lord Ashby has usefully described as the 'academic gold standard', the measure by which all Commonwealth universities are ultimately evalued.

145 By far and away the most influential model was the University of London. It provided the pattern for a string of institutions established in the 1850s in settings as diverse as Sydney, Melbourne, Calcutta, Bombay and Madras. In the twentieth century it has had an especially formative and ongoing relationship with colleges and universities in Africa and the Caribbean. Only Fourah Bay College in Sierra Leone drew upon the strictly Anglican character of the University of Durham with which it enjoyed affiliation for around a century. Beyond this, Scottish ideas of higher education have had a pervasive influence. The ideals there fostered of a general education open to all was certainly shared by the founders of universities in Australia, and they had a similar effect on the formation of some institutions in North America.

146 The eventual mixing of these models over time has meant that, for the most part, universities in the Commonwealth share recognisable features. A common base – bolstered by the kind of regular contact that is encouraged by the Association of Commonwealth Universities – has led to a situation in which students in the Commonwealth are confronted by a similar range of values enshrined in the ethos of the institutions which they attend. That is not to diminish the importance of local content or the specific influence of the broader cultural context. The English language, however, continues to be the dominant medium of instruction. And even where a political regime has tried deliberately to manipulate the university sector (as is the case irrespective of a country's stage of development), ideas of academic freedom and disinterested enquiry have persisted.

147 This is not to say that all is well with Commonwealth universities. In some cases the system of higher education is controlled by the government in order to assist in the process of realigning the position of specified sectors of the population. Access to higher education is controlled in such a way, for example, in Malaysia, where the government seeks to promote the interests of the *bumiputras* (the native born) as part of the New Economic Policy. In Sri Lanka and parts of Africa universities are closed from time to time as part of a political programme to curb opposition, while in countries like Britain and Australia university autonomy has been under threat as governments have sought to use spending controls as a way of directing universities towards areas of research and teaching that are alleged to be more 'cost effective'. This has meant that academics in the developed parts of the Commonwealth have come to share some of the experiences of their colleagues elsewhere.

Collaboration

148 Taken all in all, the tradition of Commonwealth co-operation in education has by now led to the development of collaborative programmes which embrace a substantial network of institutions and a multiplicity of academic contacts. The development of many national education systems has been assisted and promoted by the co-operative sharing of expertise and resources with other Commonwealth countries. An impressive infrastructure of co-operation exists. It deserves to be more widely known.

149 One of the most powerful of the Commonwealth's non-governmental organisations is the Association of Commonwealth Universities (ACU). The ACU has evolved from the Bureau of Information for the Universities of the Empire. Founded in 1912, it was the first body to publish the *Commonwealth Universities Yearbook*, which continues to give details of all Commonwealth universities. The bureau also ensured that one of the key resolutions of the 1912 Congress of the Universities of the Empire be fulfilled: namely 'that the universities of the various dominions of The King overseas should arrange for periodic meetings of their representatives'. The ACU now provides a well-established framework for co-operation between Commonwealth universities. With 278 member institutions in 29 countries, it organises regular meetings in different parts of the

Commonwealth. It promotes, through various schemes, the movement of academic and administrative staff; and assists the mobility of students between countries by administering, as Secretariat of the UK Commonwealth Scholarship Commission, the British part of the Commonwealth Scholarship and Fellowship Plan and other programmes.

The Commonwealth Foundation and The Commonwealth Fund for Technical Co-operation

150 We have written of both these bodies elsewhere (para. 54 and para. 231), but it is worth noting that much of the work of the former has an educational purpose, assisting many professional associations that promote education, some of which offer guidance to school-leavers and students. The CFTC provides specialist staff, including educational advisers, for governments and educational institutions, in matters concerning development.

The Education Programme of the Commonwealth Secretariat

151 The Commonwealth Secretariat's Education programme, which forms part of the Human Resources Development group, encourages and assists educational consultation and co-operation among Commonwealth countries through technical meetings, information services, research studies and training manuals, and the mobilisation of programmes and resources. It offers a modest advisory service and training experience. It promotes the study of ways of dealing with particular problems, and publishes information on educational topics. In many instances the Education Programme works in association with the Association of Commonwealth Universities, the Commonwealth Council for Educational Administration (CCEA), the Commonwealth Association of Science Technology and Mathematics Educators (CASTME), the Commonwealth Association for the Education of Adults (CAEA) and other professional associations. Most governments co-ordinate their education contacts with the Secretariat through a designated officer in the national Ministry of Education.

152 Although existing as a Commonwealth-wide scheme of scholarships, the programme is organised according to a series of

bilateral agreements. The Plan was launched in 1960 by Commonwealth governments so as to enable scholars of promise to study in countries other than their own. Thus far, close to 15,000 awards have been made. Currently about 1,800 new awards are made each year. Awards consist either of Commonwealth Scholarships for postgraduate work for research, or Commonwealth Senior Awards – professorships, fellowships – or awards for senior educational administrators. Some 30 vice-chancellors or other heads of university institutions in different parts of the Commonwealth have been Commonwealth Scholars. The Commonwealth Nassau Fellowships Scheme parallels the CSFP, and is particularly directed to any South African 'disadvantaged by apartheid' for study in appropriate education and training institutions in Commonwealth developing countries, especially in Africa.

153 Exchanges in education have long been a distinctive feature of the Commonwealth connection, contributing to the richness of its professional and institutional links. In 1982 the Commonwealth Standing Committee on Student Mobility was established in response to a widely held and deeply felt conviction that any curtailment in the movement of young people to take up study opportunities within the Commonwealth would have profound implications for the Commonwealth relationship as a whole.

154 The decline in the movement of students in the Commonwealth resulting from increases in fees payable by overseas students in key countries is still a matter for considerable concern. Commonwealth Education Ministers meeting in Nairobi in 1987

> noted with regret that the levels of intra-Commonwealth student mobility had not increased in recent years. In some countries the numbers of Commonwealth students were growing, but these cases appeared to be offset by declines elsewhere. All this was in stark contrast to the trends in some countries outside the Commonwealth, and its continuance portended a future time when cultural and intellectual ties binding the Commonwealth might be much weaker than at present. Ministers found this prospect disturbing.

155 Education Ministers in Nairobi recognised their responsibility for promoting Commonwealth student mobility by the adoption of appropriate policies. They believed that

> as a general principle, restraint by host countries in the imposition of fees and quotas, together with the provision of generous awards, would

stimulate student flows. The hope was expressed that all member countries would, in due course, give consideration to the possibility of a favourable fee regime for Commonwealth students.

156 The Commonwealth Standing Committee on Student Mobility and Higher Education Co-operation reported in June 1989 that intra-Commonwealth student mobility had apparently fallen by around 13 per cent in the previous decade, even though the four industrialised Commonwealth countries had simultaneously increased their intake of non-Commonwealth students by as much as a quarter. It was noted, however, that this compared badly with trends in other parts of the world.

157 The complementarity of Commonwealth student mobility and of efforts to promote Commonwealth higher education development have been emphasised consistently by the Commonwealth Standing Committee on Student Mobility. Strong universities, polytechnics and colleges are the key-stones of higher education development in member countries, and there is much that Commonwealth co-operation could contribute to that development. For example, new initiatives might be explored to reduce the foreign exchange problem for students abroad which might include preparatory courses at home, split-site programmes, the use of distance education and reciprocal exchange arrangements.

The Commonwealth of Learning

158 A bold new initiative by which the Commonwealth seeks to meet urgent and widespread needs for extending learning opportunities and improving educational opportunity has been taken through the establishment of the Commonwealth of Learning. This imaginative concept was developed by an expert group under the chairmanship of Lord Briggs, Provost of Worcester College, Oxford, which was set up by Commonwealth Heads of Government in 1986 to report on the potential for Commonwealth co-operation in distance education, in the light of the richness of the Commonwealth's educational resources in this area and recent advances in communications technologies. The Group's report, *Towards a Commonwealth of Learning*, set the framework for a Commonwealth agency which works through a network of existing Commonwealth colleges, universities and institutes with activities in three areas:

in the exchange, development and production of teaching materials;

in supporting individual students through the process of accreditation and credit transfer;

in institutional development of distance education.

Such a programme enables a sharing of Commonwealth teaching resources and the co-operative harnessing of communications technology to educational needs. It assists and complements conventional forms of student mobility through the sharing of teaching materials, credit transfer and support for split-site access courses.

159 The Commonwealth of Learning was formally launched with the signing of its Memorandum of Understanding in September 1988. The Headquarters are in Vancouver. Lord Briggs was elected as Chairman by the Board of Governors in November 1988. The first programmes – exchanging materials and training in distance-learning – started in 1989. The Agency does not have a large staff: it was intended that there might be 20 staff in post by the end of the first year and perhaps double that number by the end of five years. The Agency works with the regional universities of the South Pacific and the West Indies and supports regional activities in other parts of the Commonwealth. It is symbolically appropriate that the five largest donors are India, Nigeria, Britain, Brunei Darussalam and Canada. In its finances, as in its government and its work, the Commonwealth of Learning represents both developing and industrialised nations. The new institution, so far, has an income of £15 million for its first five years.

Conclusion

160 Education has made a significant contribution to the shape of the modern Commonwealth. The challenge which lies ahead is for members of the Commonwealth to harness the curative and transformative power of education in order further to develop a shared understanding which transcends borders. Many in the world look to the emergence of a new order. Few manage to realise that the model for such an order already exists in the form of the Commonwealth. As much through accident as through design, an association of nations has grown in such a way as to embrace

principles of tolerance and mutual respect. This is not to deny that there are disagreements between members – sometimes (but rarely) violent disagreements. However, it is to acknowledge that familiarity with one's neighbours, a shared language and overlapping common values may act as a restraint against overweening regional ambitions. In its promotion of fellowship and fellow-feeling the Commonwealth stands as a force for good at work in the world. Praise should not be reserved for the Commonwealth simply because it has succeeded in evolving education policies that set right some of the errors of the imperial past. We should, above all, celebrate the manner in which this has been done.

Chapter 7

WOMEN

161 Commonwealth governments are well aware of the needs and concerns of women. In the last decade a solid infrastructure has been established to aid women's development. It is hoped that in the 1990s there will be a real commitment to putting into practice many of the ideas generated in the 1980s by, and for, the benefit of women. The Anglican Communion has a crucial part to play in sharing the wealth of experience gained from its many members worldwide. Working with governments and organisations, they could make this a decade in which women are enabled to develop their full potential.

162 Commonwealth Heads of Government, since their meeting in Kingston in 1975, have regularly discussed the need for women to participate equally with men in the political, economic and social lives of their countries. At their London meeting in 1977 they concluded that:

> unless women are active participants, both contributing to the process of development and as beneficiaries, the goals of social and economic growth will not be fully realised.

The United Nations Decade for Women

163 The Decade, launched in 1976, had the aim:

> to harness international efforts to improve the lives and status of women around the world.

Agreement reached at the Commonwealth Heads of Government Meeting in Lusaka in 1979 resulted in the appointment of a Women and Development Adviser to the Secretary General. The Adviser heads a small unit to help governments and the Commonwealth Secretariat takes full account of the needs of women. In 1980, five years into the decade, United Nations statistics indicated that:

> although women constitute half the world's population, they still perform nearly two-thirds of its work hours, receive only one-tenth of its income and own less than one-hundredth of the world's property.

164 By agreeing to a UN Decade for Women it might have seemed that women's contributions were now on the agenda of their countries' planning and policy making bodies (economic and social); and that these contributions would be acknowledged, with the opportunities for women to improve their condition being greatly increased. In fact in many areas, including employment, the position of women has declined.

Decline of the position of women

165 The position of women has been adversely affected by the measures taken by governments in response to the economic crisis of the 1980s. Despite greater commitment on the part of governments towards gender issues, most women have suffered from the resulting economic and social disruption. Whilst women in the developing world suffer disproportionately, women in the old Commonwealth countries, black and white, have not escaped unscathed. With the fall in household income, a greater number of women have had to seek employment outside the home, taking poorly paid full-time jobs or part-time work. Of all part-time workers in the UK, 94 per cent are women; in Australia, the figure is 79 per cent. Further, adjustment programmes have diminished the services available to women in their non-producer role. They have been worst hit by the cuts in social services, and by the rise in morbidity and child deaths even in the so-called developed countries.

166 In Africa and the Caribbean, women have been affected by the reduction or abolition of subsidies on food and other basic goods. Per capita income has fallen by over a quarter in Sub-Saharan Africa and by about one-sixth in Latin America and the Caribbean. Women have had to cope, finding means for their families' survival, but without any assistance in their role as producers. Female headed households have been amongst the worst effected by the economic crisis with accompanying detrimental effects on their own and their children's health and education. Adjustment programmes, inevitable as a result of deteriorating terms of trade, protectionism by developing countries, high rates of interest and slower growth in world trade, were designed without consideration for the poor. No account was taken of women's specific needs and concerns. These programmes have caused severe hardship and much damage to the human and capital resources available to society.

167 In addition to being economic producers, most women are home managers, child bearers, and carers of children and the elderly. They are also involved with men as community organisers. As a result, women work longer hours than men, but with fewer resources, often little or no opportunity for advancement and far lower rewards than men. Women's role as producer has been crucial to the survival of poor families over the last decade. This has led to a need for more child-care facilities which has not been fulfilled. To meet growing demand private nurseries and day-care centres have mushroomed; with government run nurseries offering part-time provision, a large part of women's earnings have gone to pay for child care.

168 Worldwide, female-headed households and the elderly (a greater proportion of whom are women) constitute the largest poverty group. In Australia 75 per cent of all people living in poverty are women or children under the age of 18 years; in Canada 60 per cent of all women over the age of 65 live in poverty. Women who are solely responsible for their families often cannot go out to work because there are no child-care facilities available, or because child care is too expensive. Invariably when they do go out to work they get paid less than men, and have fewer prospects for climbing the promotional ladder. The reason for this is probably linked to the uncertainties of marriage and child-rearing; to lower self-esteem, and the acceptance of the male career as being more important. Women may also be less involved in union activities, have less representation at decision-making level or, as has been suggested, are less willing to extol their own strengths at job interviews.

Structural Adjustment policies

169 Given the conditions (described in paras 165 to 167), it is not surprising that when the Commonwealth Ministers responsible for women's affairs met for the first time in 1985 they identified the impact of Structural Adjustment policies on women as a priority issue. They met again in Zimbabwe in 1987 and recommended that an expert group be established:

to identify the extent of the contribution of women to different economies;

to examine the evidence of the impact on women of Structural Adjustment measures;

to consider alternatives which would be socially and economically effective in enhancing the position of women.

170 A plan of action on Women and Development was endorsed in Vancouver later in that year. One of its main objectives is to promote gender issues and to ensure that women are involved in the policy-making and decision-making processes of their countries. A report from the Expert Group states:

> The essence of women's distinctiveness lies in the multiplicity of their roles.... Adjustment policies which fail to incorporate women's concerns fully, are not only unjust and cause unnecessary hardship, but also imperil the effectiveness of the policies themselves.

Undervaluing of women

171 Women's contributions are continually undervalued. Although, as already stated, two-thirds of the world's work is done by women phrases such as 'the integration of women into development', or 'enhancing the contribution of women to development' are often used. There still exists the notion that the unpaid work that women do (in the home and in agriculture) is less valuable than the work done by their men. At the 1985 Review of the United Nations Decade of Women in Nairobi, a declaration was passed which stated, inter alia, that:

> To benefit women, development must be defined by women. Either by themselves or in co-operation with men, women must first address the obstacle to their own development; with newly gained skills and confidence they can then turn to the task of development for the entire community.

Women's initiatives

172 In 1978 a group of middle class women in India founded the Working Forum. At first they offered loans and support to women. Later they explored other areas; health care, family planning and legal assistance. The emphasis was always placed on the women gaining confidence, raising self-esteem and empowering them to make changes in their lives. The Forum proved a tremendous success. In September, 1986, biologist Wangura Maathai received an award from the Better World Society for starting Kenya's Green Belt Movement. The Movement has planted over two million trees in Kenya. Another example of women's potential for improving the environment, the CHIPCO (tree hugging) Movement in India has women banding

together to protect fuel and fodder resources from lumberjacks. In Canada women protest against uranium mining, and at Greenham Common in England, women helped set off a wave of protest right across Europe against the installation of Cruise missiles by the United States.

Women as victims

173 In common with women throughout the world, Commonwealth women are subject to expressions of male dominance including domestic violence. Rosalind Coward writes:

> Men's attitude to sex and to women's bodies, the fear of possible violence from men and the characteristic male emotional responses .... are all factors which colour women's everyday experience of the world but which do not derive from any direct economic oppression. And many of these problems are just as present in the behaviour of sympathetic men as in men hostile to the whole idea of feminism.

174 AIDS is now the leading cause of death in women aged 20 to 40 in Western Europe, the Americas and sub-Saharan Africa. In the poorest countries of the developing world, where women have little economic independence and poverty puts them at greater risk of HIV infection, there is resulting evidence of the vicious impact of AIDS on families and national economies. Only programmes that address women's lack of power and social status will help control the spread of HIV in those countries where women are so vulnerable to infection.

175 There is also a violence which takes the form of racism and, like sexism, it is used to isolate women. It has been effective in fragmenting the struggles of women – both black and white – and preventing them from recognising and understanding the common experience and proper inheritance of all women. The Commonwealth, peopled as it is by black and white, rich and poor, must have a special role in the confrontation and erosion of racism.

Marginalisation

176 Too many women are still marginalised. Religious and cultural doctrines continue to emphasise that women's primary responsibility is to the home and family. Change and progress, however, has meant that there is a need for women to opt to work outside the home: to

support their country's economy as well as their own families. Thus today's women find themselves being pressured to be both full-time carers and fully committed producers. Certainly women should have the right to choose to work outside the home, or to work within the home as home-makers. Commonwealth Heads of Government, meeting in Kuala Lumpur in 1989, stressed the importance of adopting policies which would facilitate women's full participation in the public and private sectors. They emphasised the need to redress the socio-economic inequalities facing women, and the importance of women's access to education, training, credit, land and employment.

Women in leadership

177 Some Commonwealth countries have chosen women as their leaders, which has been valuable in affirming the status of women. Among the earliest women Prime Ministers were Mrs Bandaranaike of Sri Lanka (formerly Ceylon) and Mrs Indira Gandhi of India. Other countries have followed suit with, most recently, Margaret Thatcher as Prime Minister of Britain for eleven and a half years; and Benazir Bhutto as Prime Minister of Pakistan for a much briefer period. A considerable number of Commonwealth countries have women in key Government ministries and in the diplomatic corps women are to be found as High Commissioners/Ambassadors.

178 The Anglican Communion is only now going through the process (though somewhat more painfully) which many other institutions have experienced of having women in positions of leadership, in its decisions over women priests and bishops. The Episcopal Church in the United States of America was the first to elect a woman, Bishop Barbara Harris, as a suffragan Bishop in 1989, followed in 1990 by the election in the Church of the Province of New Zealand of Bishop Penelope Jamieson as Bishop of the diocese of Dunedin. By 1990 there were a growing number of provinces in the Anglican Communion in which women were serving as clergy, although in some the office of priest is, as yet, closed to them.

The Lambeth Conference and women

179 It is however important to note that at the Lambeth Conference in 1988 there was more acknowledgement of the contribution of

women in the Anglican Communion. One plenary session was a presentation by women, relating to women and the themes of the Conference. In addition one of the responses to the Archbishop of Canterbury's opening address was given by Elizabeth Templeton who was one of six women consultants, and the assistant to the Chaplain was a woman. Of course women were present in many other capacities and the Conference Secretariat was staffed almost entirely by women – and without the Secretariat the Conference would not have survived!

180 A lively and much appreciated Wives' Conference was held during the Lambeth Conference for the first time. Inevitably the visibility of these women alongside those mentioned in para. 181 enabled Lambeth 1988 to appear much less of a 'men only' event. In Resolution 34 on Marriage and Family para. 4d the Conference resolved to

> recognise that these pressures (political, economic and social pressures on family life) serve to diminish the economic well-being and status of women, welcomes the World Council of Churches 'Decade for Solidarity with Women', and encourages dioceses to consider how they might through their theological, structural and pastoral approaches help to achieve a fuller recognition of the contribution and status of women in Church and society.

Lack of response to WCC initiative

181 Despite this resolution the Ecumenical Decade 1988-1998: *Churches in Solidarity with Women* has had as yet a rather patchy response from the Anglican Communion. In many Provinces it is groups of women at local level, rather than Church structures at national level, who are trying to encourage serious observance of the Decade. The exception is in the Provinces of the Americas where plans are well advanced in the organisation of a conference to be held in Brazil in 1992. This seems likely to be the major Anglican Communion response to the World Council of Churches' initiative.

Chapter 8

IMMIGRATION

The slave trade

182 International trade and politics led to the movement of peoples. The history of the British Empire and latterly, of the Commonwealth, is no exception. One of the saddest features of this history was the trade in people between the seventeenth and nineteenth centuries – the slave trade. Vast numbers of people were taken, against their will, from their homes in Africa to provide cheap slave labour for other parts of the world. In the process multitudes perished and multitudes of others suffered profound and wicked abuse of their humanity. Thus African peoples went to the West Indies, to the United States of America, to South America and to Europe. The main beneficiaries of this immoral and cruel trade were the colonial powers and the US.

183 A prolonged campaign in the latter part of the eighteenth century and into the early years of the nineteenth century led first to the abolition of slavery in Britain and then to the outlawing of the whole slave trade. The history of this struggle is well documented and has been written up in full both from the point of view of black communities struggling for freedom and of those white people who viewed the practice of slavery with moral and religious repugnance.

UK immigrants

184 It is important that this history is remembered. This is especially so in coming to any understanding of the significance of the experience of our times in restricting immigration into the UK and in closely defining the legal meaning of nationality in Britain. Many of the people who sought, after the end of the Second World War, to take up their rights as citizens of the UK and Colonies and make their homes in the UK, came from communities whose origins were in the slave trade. They were where they were by the enforced actions of the British in earlier centuries. The raw, and racist reactions of some in

calls to 'send them home' are totally insensitive to the history of British racism rooted, as it is, in the history of slavery and the slave trade and in that of indentured labour.

185 These reactions are made even more insensitive by the recalling of the motivation for post-war immigration into Britain of people from black communities in the new Commonwealth. Post-war Britain surprised itself. The experience of the 1920s and '30s had been a grim one of persistent unemployment and misery in traditional working-class communities. The fear of the 1920s and '30s dominated the political scene in the establishment of the pattern of post-war economic and political expectation. During the war years economists sought to forecast the likely pattern of unemployment once the war was over. Expectations ranged from six per cent to 13 per cent of the available work force. In reality post-war Britain experienced the lowest levels of unemployment ever recorded. The national figure hovered around the two per cent level for the decade following 1945. Britain experienced a considerable labour shortage both in the private industrial sector in manual work and in the public sector especially in the less skilled jobs. This led to employers, in both the public and private sector, actively seeking labour overseas in the colonies and the new nations of the Commonwealth. One of the primary reasons why people came to Britain from the West Indies and the Indian sub-continent was that they were actively recruited to come. Once the bandwagon was moving, indicating that Britain needed their labour, people began to come in significant numbers. Again, that part of our history in actively seeking black labour for British industry and public service is often forgotten in debate about immigration policy.

186 The story of the way black people experienced life in Britain once they had arrived is well-known. It makes sorry reading. Our immediate experience of racism is centred on the arrival and settlement of black people from the new Commonwealth. The resident white community, in the main, saw black people as a threat, treated them as inferior beings, and discriminated against them in jobs, housing, education and general social experience. The Church, with rare exceptions, proved to be no different. Anglicans, Baptists, Methodists and Roman Catholics coming from the West Indies and the Indian sub-continent found their respective churches in Britain unwelcoming and unprepared to integrate them into their life and mission.

187 The difficulties were of sufficient seriousness to lead to riots, as in Nottingham and Notting Hill in the autumn of 1958, and to a feeling of social conflict and hostility in some of our urban communities. Black people were clearly unwelcome to large numbers of white British citizens.

188 This is the background of public policy for immigration and for race relations within Britain. The detailed story of the legislation process has been set out on a number of occasions by church bodies including the General Synod. It is not our purpose to go over the detail once again. Our task is to look at the direction and trend of policy and what it means in the setting of our commitment to the Commonwealth.

Direction and trend of immigration policy

189 The more encouraging side of policy has been the attempt at tackling discrimination on grounds of race within the UK. Successive Race Relations Acts have made it unlawful to discriminate against people on grounds of their race in matters such as employment, social life, education and housing. The efforts of successive administrations in the UK have been criticised for failing to ensure that the institutions set up to tackle discrimination have been adequately resourced for the task. That includes criticism of the failure to ensure that those who carry power in different sections of our corporate life have often, themselves, not received any training or scrutiny as to their competence in their sphere. Nevertheless, the mechanism of the law has been and continues to be used to try to reduce and outlaw acts of racial discrimination. The persistent evidence of the continued disadvantage experienced by black people in Britain in all spheres of our common life indicate that there is still much work to be done. In a survey for *The Independent* (April 1990) over the proposed admission of Hong Kong Chinese, people were asked whether Britain could absorb more of particular groups. With regard to the admission of Indians and Pakistanis, 84 per cent said no; of West Indians 83 per cent; of Chinese 77 per cent; of Jews 67 per cent; of other Europeans 60 per cent; of white Commonwealth 54 per cent.

190 The other side of public policy has been much more controversial and is less encouraging. At one and the same time as attempts have been made to reduce discrimination on grounds of race within Britain,

by both legislative and administrative means, efforts have been made to restrict severely immigration into the UK from the new Commonwealth. Since this latter arm of policy appears to have been aimed specifically at restricting the entry of black people into Britain, it sits uneasily with policies designed to tackle racial discrimination.

191 The law on immigration is established in the 1962, 1968 and 1973 Acts of Parliament. Progressively, these have sought to make it more difficult for people to enter Britain for permanent settlement. These Acts established both the philosophy and procedures for immigration practice. The actual process of immigration is governed by the Immigration rules, which, like the Acts of Parliament, have become progressively more severe at every stage.

'Patrials' and 'non-patrials'

192 If the 1962 Act set the process moving, the 1968 and 1973 Acts established the principles and practice of all subsequent immigration policy. In terms of principle the crucial distinction, made in this legislation, concerns the difference between 'patrial' and 'non-patrial' persons. Patrial persons are those who can demonstrate a close connection with the UK. That is defined in relational terms. People whose parents or grandparents were born in Britain are considered patrial people and have a right of entry for settlement into the UK. All other citizens of the Commonwealth, who until the passing of these laws had a right of entry, lost that right when they were defined as non-patrial. In effect this meant that people, predominantly from the old white Commonwealth, retained their historic access to the UK since many could demonstrate patriality. Those from the non-white new Commonwealth who, in the main, did not qualify as patrial people lost the right of access to the UK. Thus it appeared that the law set out to discriminate in favour of white people with British connections and against black people, even if they were in possession of a passport for the UK and Colonies. The legislation was clearly designed to halt the immigration into the UK of people from the new Commonwealth. Black people have experienced it as racist discrimination. Those white people who view racism with as much repugnance as abolitionists regarded slavery have fought such legislation.

193 This distinction between patrial and non-patrial citizens has formed the basis for subsequent nationality legislation. The British Nationality Act 1981 which came into force in 1983 used it as a basis for establishing categories of people who would be required both to apply for British nationality and to pay for it in the process. Thus, those people who had successfully entered the UK as citizens of the UK and Colonies found themselves being required to have to apply and pay for something which they considered they already possessed. Clearly the establishment of the independence and separate nationality of former colonies meant that attention needed to be given to British nationality law. However, the method chosen for achieving this, rooted as it was in the principles established in Immigration Law, was seen as racist. Once again, a predominantly black community found itself being made to feel on the margins of British society. It ought to have been possible to enable those who entered the UK under the 1948 provisions, once their own nations of origin had established their own independence, to have their nationality and citizenship position normalised as British, if they so chose, without the complication which the 1981 Act required. Added to this the Home Office made inadequate provision for implementing the Act, leading to people experiencing considerable personal inconvenience through the delays which occurred.

Hong Kong

194 Similar feelings have been aroused over the problems associated with the transfer of Hong Kong to China in 1997. The 1981 Act cut the people of Hong Kong off from any right of entry into the UK. Their citizenship under the Dependent Territories provision gave no right of entry into Britain on a permanent basis. The re-emergence of open repression in China, following the Tiananmen Square riots, added to the anxieties of the people of Hong Kong concerning the future. The consequent provision for a limited number of people from Hong Kong, chosen on the basis of their financial or professional status to be able to settle into Britain, if they so chose, was an attempt by the British Government to relieve fears. The not-too-hidden fears in the minds of many in Britain concerned the possibility that large numbers of Hong Kong Chinese might come to Britain permanently. Again, overt racist attitudes surfaced as it became clear that it was the thought of *Chinese* people arriving here which aroused alarm. It proved

difficult for HMG to establish the view that some provision of access to the UK would help stabilise the situation in Hong Kong and help people there, who had no real desire to leave, to plan to stay in the knowledge that the 1997 transfer would not cut them off from the rest of the world. (para. 82).

Stricter rules for the Commonwealth: liberal provisions within the EC

195 Since the 1981 Act, the immigration rules have become even more difficult. We have witnessed the distress of people from Sri Lanka fleeing civil strife there and the refusal of the authorities to countenance them as refugees. The Government refuses at present to consider setting up an in-country right of appeal for those denied asylum before they are returned to their country of origin, though pressed by refugee organisations to do so. Every move made by Government seems designed to shut the door to black people who may wish to enter the UK to join their families already settled here. All of this is made much more difficult for people to accept as they watch the provisions within the EC made more and more liberal. This is symbolised by the change in the British passport which is no longer a passport of the UK and Colonies but a passport specifically provided for the open frontiers of the European Community. People from across the Community may move freely within its borders whilst people from the Commonwealth, who do not have patrial status, have no rights of permanent entry, even in many cases to join their families.

Need for change in present laws

196 If the Commonwealth is to have any meaning as a community of diverse peoples and cultures then Immigration and Nationality Law should be equitable to all Commonwealth citizens. The distinction between patrial and non-patrial people has proved to be disastrous in the perception of white as well as black people. Moreover, for those who have successfully settled into the UK there must be easy access for their own families to join them. The normal concerns of people for the care of their close and elderly relatives should be sympathetically provided for. Few would wish to suggest that it is possible these days to have a policy of no restriction. It is certainly true that the move from Colonial Status to Independence required an adjustment of British

policy to take account of the new realities. Such changes, however, *must be seen to be non-racist in practice.* The history of British policy in this area, pursued by Governments of all persuasions – supported by large sections of public opinion – has not been good. The Churches have been right to challenge it on religious and ethical grounds. The continued existence and life of the Commonwealth offer one way in which these matters can be set in a new context of commitment to the value of multi-cultural and diverse communities – to the concept of one world shared by all its people under God its Creator and Redeemer.

Chapter 9

APARTHEID

197 International groupings whether of nations or Churches are subject to strains and tensions. The Commonwealth and the Anglican Communion are no exceptions. In the Commonwealth there have been, over the last few years, a number of these disagreements: Pakistan left the Commonwealth, returning in 1989; Fiji's membership has lapsed; the civil war in Sri Lanka has caused difficulty with India and Britain. However the longest and most difficult problem between Britain and other members of the Commonwealth has been that of apartheid in South Africa. This difficulty has not, however, been seriously mirrored between the Church of England and the Anglican Communion, rather it has been reflected in relationships between the Church of England and the British Government over the last decade.

Background

198 As explained in Chapter 3 'Britain in the Commonwealth' by 1960 the attention of the Commonwealth was being focused on South Africa. Just six weeks before the 1960 Prime Ministers' Meeting, the killing at Sharpeville of 69 Africans peacefully demonstrating against the apartheid system aroused world-wide revulsion. South Africa's application that year for continued membership of the Commonwealth after the country became a republic provided an opportunity for consideration of the nature of its policies. The apartheid issue dominated the meeting. The communiqué of the meeting affirmed that equality of race within member states was as vital to the Commonwealth as equality between member states.

199 Further condemnation of apartheid policies at the 1961 Prime Ministers' Meeting led to South Africa's withdrawal of its application to continue in the Commonwealth. In 1974 South Africa was suspended from participation in the United Nations General Assembly.

200 The Heads of Government at their meeting in London in 1977 widened the mandate of the Commonwealth Committee on Sanctions (which had been set up in 1966 to support and monitor the implementation of sanctions against Rhodesia) in recognition of the interrelated nature of the problems of Southern Africa. The Committee was renamed the Commonwealth Committee on Southern Africa. The Committee has remained a major forum for Commonwealth Consultation and diplomatic interaction on Southern African issues, reporting biennially to Heads of Government.

Gleneagles Agreement

201 With the Gleneagles Agreement in 1977 Commonwealth leaders sought to cut the sporting connection. Member governments agreed 'to combat the evil of apartheid by withholding any form of support for, and by taking every practical step to discourage contact or competition by their nationals with sporting organisations, teams or sportsmen from South Africa or from any other country where sports are organised on the basis of race, colour or ethnic origin.'

202 The Agreement had an immediate and significant effect in diminishing sporting contacts with South Africa. Moreover, six months later the UN General Assembly adopted the International Declaration against Apartheid in Sports, imposing a worldwide boycott on sporting links with South Africa. The overwhelming majority of countries had no official sporting contacts with the Pretoria regime in 1990.

203 By March 1991 golf and soccer had unified sports bodies and negotiations were underway to form a non-racial organisation for South African cricket. The white governing bodies of tennis and rugby had been slower to move in this direction.

204 Outside the Gleneagles framework, strong feelings against apartheid adversely affected a major Commonwealth sporting event, the 1986 Commonwealth Games in Edinburgh, Scotland. Despite efforts by the Commonwealth Secretary-General to resolve the problem, 32 of the 58 Commonwealth Games Federation affiliates withdrew from the Games in protest at the British Government's reluctance to impose wide-ranging economic sanctions against

Pretoria in line with other Commonwealth governments. Happily the 1990 Commonwealth Games in Auckland were not similarly disrupted, although the English rebel cricket tour did threaten them.

Popular resistance in South Africa

205 The mid-1970s marked a turning point in the struggle against apartheid. Within South Africa, there was an upsurge of popular resistance – the rejection by young black people of the inferior education offered to them, growing militancy in the workplace, more outspoken condemnation by black church and community leaders, and signs of renewed guerrilla activity by the nationalist movements. Internationally, South Africa faced an increasingly hostile environment.

206 Commonwealth Heads of Government at New Delhi in 1983 authorised Commonwealth action, in co-operation with the UN, to disseminate the truth about apartheid and about the social and economic progress in African countries. Consultations between the Commonwealth Committee on Southern Africa, the Secretariat and the UN Centre Against Apartheid led to the formulation of a Commonwealth programme to complement UN action. The mandate was renewed at the 1985 Commonwealth summit in Nassau.

207 In his 1985 report, Shridath Ramphal, the Commonwealth Secretary-General, pointed to the importance of sanctions against apartheid but also addressed opinion opposed to sanctions:

> They use two main arguments. First, that sanctions will not work, quoting the experience of sanctions against the Smith regime in Southern Rhodesia but ignoring that South Africa was there to serve the Rhodesian regime as a conduit for trade in breach of the quarantine. Second, that sanctions will hurt South Africa's black majority more than its white oppressors, a touching concern which ignores that those blacks in South Africa who most want an end to apartheid, from Nelson Mandela downwards, have made it pellucidly clear that they are for sanctions. They know that sanctions will hurt immeasurably less than either apartheid's continued violence against them or the conflict that will be required to uproot it in the absence of sanctions.
>
> But there is another side to sanctions, less talked about. Countries which have invested most in South Africa and trade most with South Africa have a greater adjustment to make if sanctions are imposed – but they also have a greater moral responsibility to impose them: for, by the level of their

economic involvement they underwrite apartheid, however much they may dislike it. To sustain that involvement and resist sanctions when everyone else is wishing to impose them comes close to becoming an accomplice in apartheid. It is a serious matter for all Commonwealth countries – and the Commonwealth.

208 As the Heads of Government met in Nassau in 1985 worldwide condemnation of Pretoria's internal repression and external aggression heightened. In their Nassau Accord, Commonwealth leaders unanimously declared that 'South Africa's continuing refusal to dismantle apartheid, its illegal occupation of Namibia, and its aggression against its neighbours constitute a serious challenge to the values and principles of the Commonwealth, a challenge which Commonwealth countries cannot ignore'.

They therefore called on the South African Government to take five specific steps:

i) Declare that the system of apartheid will be dismantled and meaningful action taken in fulfilment of that intent.

ii) Terminate the existing state of emergency.

iii) Release immediately and unconditionally Nelson Mandela and all others imprisoned and detained for their opposition to apartheid.

iv) Establish political freedom and specifically lift the existing ban on the African National Congress and other political parties.

v) Initiate, in the context of a suspension of violence on all sides, a process of dialogue across lines of colour, politics and religion, with a view to establishing a non-racial and representative government.

The Heads of Government:

decided to set up a group of eminent Commonwealth persons to facilitate such a dialogue;

agreed on a series of nine economic measures to signal their opposition to apartheid, including bans on loans to South Africa, the sale and export of computer equipment to the South African security forces, and the sale and export of oil and of nuclear goods and technology to South Africa;

decided that the President of Zambia and the Prime Ministers of Australia, the Bahamas, Britain, Canada, India and Zimbabwe should review the position after six months and, in the absence of sufficient progress, the leaders would consider further measures of economic pressure.

209 The urgent need for action against pro-apartheid propaganda was heightened by the sweeping curbs placed on the press in South Africa, the severest ever imposed there, under the nationwide June 1986 state of emergency, renewed and strengthened a year later. South Africa's restrictions on media reporting were now among the harshest in the world. Contraventions were punished by prison sentences for local journalists and expulsions for the foreign press. In January 1987 even blank spaces in newspapers were forbidden; it was also illegal to express any support in speech or writing for the release of those detained under the emergency regulations. The regime tried to use the emergency regulations to substitute pro-apartheid propaganda in place of independent news reporting.

The Commonwealth Eminent Persons' Group

210 The Commonwealth Eminent Persons' Group entrusted with carrying out the task of helping to initiate a dialogue with the South African regime, appointed by the Secretary-General, comprised six men and one woman: Malcolm Fraser of Australia and General Olusegun Obasanjo of Nigeria (co-chairmen), Lord Barbour (Britain), Dame Nita Barrow (Barbados), John Malecela (Tanzania), Sardar Swaran Singh (India) and Archbishop Edward Scott (Canada).

211 The Group's report was made public in London by the two co-chairmen on 12 June 1986, under the title *Mission to South Africa: The Commonwealth Report*. The report records the Group's eventual failure, following their gradual gaining of the confidence of both sides and the hopes raised among people, both black and white, in South Africa and beyond.

212 The seven Commonwealth leaders nominated in the Nassau Accord met in London in August 1986 to review the South African situation and to consider the report of the Eminent Persons' Group. In their Communiqué, they warmly commended the EPG for its 'positive and enduring contribution to the efforts to end apartheid and establish a non-racial and representative government in South Africa'. They agreed that Pretoria had taken none of the five steps called for at Nassau, that there had not been adequate concrete progress towards

ending apartheid, and indeed the situation had deteriorated. They therefore considered the adoption of further measures to persuade Pretoria to dismantle apartheid and install the structures of democracy.

213 All the seven leaders agreed that further sanctions should be applied but differed on the nature of the sanctions to be taken. Britain alone dissented from adopting the further set of wide-ranging measures envisaged in the Nassau Accord, as well as certain additional measures and to commend them to the rest of the Commonwealth. The other leaders stated that if these further measures did not have the desired effect within a reasonable time, still further measures would have to be considered.

Vancouver Statement

214 The Commonwealth Heads of Government Meeting held in Vancouver some 15 months later warmly commended the work of the Eminent Persons' Group. They agreed that the group's mission to South Africa and its 'negotiating concept' had offered a real opportunity for the launching of a process leading to what they called 'a peaceful resolution of the problem of apartheid and to a break in the cycle of violence in the region'. The rejection by Pretoria of the 'negotiating concept' was they said 'nothing less than tragic'. Pretoria however, had destroyed the group's work by attacking neighbouring Commonwealth countries of Botswana, Zambia and Zimbabwe on 19 May 1986. Commonwealth leaders at Vancouver again called on the South African Government to accept the 'negotiating concept', which was still valid, as the best way to avert catastrophe through negotiations.

215 At Vancouver in 1987 the Commonwealth, deeply concerned at the continuing deterioration in the situation in South Africa, issued the Okanagan Statement. This statement summarised the discussions of the meeting relating to Southern Africa. But the divide between Britain and the rest of the Commonwealth was highlighted. At each point that related to current sanctions and their tightening, the phrase, 'with the exception of Britain' was inserted. More happily there was complete agreement on action in Southern Africa to assist the Front Line States, particularly Mozambique, and increasing humanitarian and legal assistance to victims and opponents of apartheid.

216 The Vancouver meeting set up the Commonwealth Committee of Foreign Ministers on Southern Africa (Australia, Canada, Guyana, India, Nigeria, Tanzania and Zimbabwe) to provide a high-level impetus and guidance to the whole Commonwealth strategy. Britain dissented from the setting up of this Committee. Between Vancouver and Kuala Lumpur the Committee met on four occasions to monitor developments in South Africa and with continuing evidence of deterioration there, they imposed further sanctions. They also published two reports: one on South Africa's relationship with the international financial system and one on destabilisation of the Front Line States by South Africa.

Kuala Lumpur: Britain still at odds

217 Meeting in Kuala Lumpur in 1989 the Commonwealth Heads of Government discussed many topics of common interest on which they agreed. However, South Africa and particularly sanctions continued to divide Britain from the rest of the Commonwealth as they had done at Nassau and Vancouver.

218 Reports were received from various expert groups, mainly relating to sanctions and financial links with South Africa. One however dealt with the issue of the destabilisation of the Front Line States by South Africa. These reports assisted the Heads of Government in their review of the situation. They noted that, despite some progress, Nelson Mandela, the Deputy President of the African National Congress, was still in prison, after 27 years; that the African National Congress (ANC), the Pan-Africanist Congress (PAC) and other political organisations were still banned and that the major pillars of apartheid were still in place.

219 The tone of the Kuala Lumpur Statement was one of very cautious optimism but once more Britain found itself at odds with all the other members of the Commonwealth. At each point in the Statement where action relating to sanctions are mentioned the qualification *other than Britain* or *with the exception of Britain* is added.

Release of Nelson Mandela

220 In a speech on 2 February 1990 President de Klerk announced that Nelson Mandela would be released from prison. He was subsequently

released on 11 February to the acclaim of the whole international community.

221 As well as the release of Mr Mandela, President de Klerk announced a number of other steps towards a new South Africa including:

lifting restrictions on the African National Congress, the Pan-Africanist Congress, the South African Communist Party and over 30 other oppostion organisations

releasing of (what he termed) genuine political prisoners

rescinding of restrictions on 33 organisations.

222 These measures were received in different ways by Britain and the other members of the Commonwealth. Britain sought to persuade its partners in the European Community to begin to lift sanctions and in February 1990 unilaterally lifted its ban on new investments and tourism. The Commonwealth Committee of Foreign Ministers (para. 216) meeting in Nigeria in May 1990, however, declared that 'now is not the time to lift sanctions against South Africa'.

223 On 1 February 1991 President de Klerk announced significant changes in National Party policy including the repeal of the Land Acts, the Group Areas Act and the Population Registration Act. Meeting on 16 February in London the Commonwealth Committee of Foreign Ministers on Southern Africa reported that their firm view was that it was 'crucial to maintain sanctions.... up to and including the adoption of a new constitution'.

The future

224 As the Working Party finished its work, despite the continual struggle for democracy in South Africa, cautious optimism about the future of South Africa is apparent. If this cautious optimism is indeed the correct assessment in March 1991, then a chapter of tension between Britain and the rest of the Commonwealth will finally end. Hopefully the end will be a beginning with the re-entry of South Africa as the fifty-first member of the Commonwealth.

Chapter 10

RICH AND POOR

225 The Commonwealth recognises the disparities of wealth among its partners. It is not a homogeneous group and there are conflicts of economic interest. But bilaterally, regionally and as an institution, it works to produce research, aid and networks that address in a practical way the issues of rich and poor, particularly in their unique manifestations in Commonwealth countries. Two Commonwealth institutions have been established to boost investment in developing nation members.

The Commonwealth Development Corporation

226 'The new word for peace', wrote Pope Pius VI, 'is development.' The Commonwealth Development Corporation (CDC) is a UK statutory body established in 1947 and charged with the task of assisting overseas countries in the development of their economies. Its brief permits it to operate in Britain's remaining dependencies and any other Commonwealth or developing country through the provision of debt and equity for projects, management for projects and resources and ancillary services like purchasing, marketing and personnel related to projects. Some three-quarters of CDC's £1.2 billion investments and commitments to invest are in Commonwealth countries.

227 Funded from Britain's aid budget at concessional rates that it passes on to its borrowers, CDC is a conduit of Official Development Assistance (ODA); but the organisation is run on corporate lines making direct investments (i.e. shares) in projects from which it receives profits and on which it may realise gains when it sells the investments on.

228 Nearly a third of CDC's investments by value have been made in the small island states of the Caribbean and Pacific. South and South-East Asia account for a similar amount and the remainder has been

directed towards Africa. While half of its funds have gone into primary production and processing development (mostly agriculture and forestry) just over a third have been committed to basic infrastructural development such as communication and transport. The remaining £200 million has been deployed in industrial and commercial ventures.

Commonwealth Equity Fund

229 A more recent development is the effort sponsored by the Secretariat to channel private institutional equity investment into the Commonwealth's developing countries. It came to fruition in September 1990 with the launch of the Commonwealth Equity Fund (CEF). The CEF's origins lay in an idea that Finance Ministers took up after their annual meeting in 1988. Investors from North America and Europe (including the International Finance Corporation – the equity investment arm of the World Bank) have placed nearly $60 million with the CEF which in turn hopes, with the assistance of the Commonwealth Secretariat, to gain access to the small emerging stock markets of the Commonwealth's developing nations.

230 There are only seven aid donors among the Commonwealth's membership. Some, like New Zealand, choose to focus their programmes regionally with the result that a large proportion is disbursed to Pacific Island states that also happen to belong to the Commonwealth.

Commonwealth Fund for Technical Co-operation

231 The Commonwealth-wide effort at providing aid to its own assumes the form of the Commonwealth Fund for Technical Co-operation (CFTC). The CFTC maintains a register of some 5,000 technical experts – the majority from developing countries – to offer project, consultancy and training services. Two-thirds of the fund's work is in small and other specially disadvantaged states – often in conjunction with other multilateral organisations. Voluntary contributions from Commonwealth members provide the fund's budget which in 1991 is about £30 million per annum. In addition to the range of projects related to industry, health, finance, education, agriculture, energy, trade, transport and communications the fund

has two programmes, funded by earmarked rather than general contributions, concerned with Southern Africa. Mozambique, a non-Commonwealth country, is the subject of one on account of its strategic geographical relationship to front line states.

Local initiatives

232 Under academic and other sponsorship, there have also been a number of regional meetings designed to address local economic issues. For example, the Australian National University and the World Bank held a workshop on investment possibilities in the small island states of the Pacific. The Commonwealth states of the Caribbean and Africa have separately held symposia on adjustment policies. The Caribbean states furthered their discussions towards the harmonisation of regional exchange rates and policies and have conferred about a co-ordinating economic policy for their region by the end of the century.

233 Commonwealth countries work within a number of global, regional and disciplinary fora to analyse and tackle the problems of rich and poor; they also approach a wide range of economic issues in a Commonwealth context. Rather than attempting to replicate the work of larger and better resourced international organisations, their approach is often tailored to the unique problems of their membership e.g. refugees in Africa, small island states, territories prone to natural disasters, regional co-operative resource management, the need for new and renewable sources of energy to reduce the oil imports and the effects of that commodity's price changes. Nonetheless, even though Commonwealth countries form only a small part of the group under pressure from extreme and unsustainable debt burdens, in 1990 the British Chancellor chose to unveil his proposals for debt rescheduling to the Commonwealth Finance Ministers at their annual meeting that precedes the IMF gathering.

234 Much debate has taken place since Britain joined the European Community as to whether or not this weakens her ties with the Commonwealth. Whilst it would be foolish not to acknowledge that there have been some strains, it is important to note that Britain has the possibility to act as an interpreter between the European Community and a large world organisation – the Commonwealth. Britain also has the privileged position of being in association through

the Commonwealth with a number of key countries in the developing grouping of Pacific nations, a region which is becoming increasingly important economically.

Trade

235 35 of the 67 developing nations (together the ACP – Africa, Caribbean, Pacific – group) that join twelve EC countries in the Lomé Convention are Commonwealth members. As signatories, they benefit from the aid priorities of the European members as well as from preferential trade access terms. The Commonwealth participants jointly negotiated access to the EC under the convention. Recently, a fifth generation of the convention was signed to extend for ten years to 1999 thus covering the crucial period of full European integration in 1992 and of Eastern Europe's economic liberalisation.

236 At the same time that developing countries strive to pay their way through trade, the Commonwealth's industrialised members are also lobbying on their own behalf against the protectionist barriers that obstruct their ability to sell their products competitively. In this respect, Australia and New Zealand share with the developing nations the difficulties of diversifying markets for their commodity agricultural exports.

237 The Commonwealth as an institution takes a vigorous stand in support of a successful conclusion of the talks known as the Uruguay Round – negotiations under the auspices of the General Agreement on Tariff and Trade. In addition to the individual voices in support of a freer structure for international trade, its secretariat has staffed an observer at the talks and written extensive briefs for members.

Disparities within the Commonwealth

238 There are institution-wide, regional and thematic examples of co-operation within the Commonwealth. It is worth putting them in context with the size of the Commonwealth and the disparities in economic condition of its members. 43 of the Commonwealth countries are developing. They range from India with 800 million citizens to Tuvalu with 8,000. According to the World Bank series, the Commonwealth's poorest country was Bangladesh with $160 GNP per capita. Seven industrialised nations are Commonwealth

members, including Britain and Canada which belong to the most exclusive bracket of wealthy and economically powerful nations, the G7. Their citizens' output at $10,420 and $15,160 per capita respectively in 1987 were multiples of most other Commonwealth peoples'.

239 The economic profiles and performances of Commonwealth nations are as diverse as any group of countries – but the 50 members include a disproportionate number of poor and very small states. They nevertheless have some very specific economic problems. They also share with their wealthier Commonwealth partners common concern for such matters as the economic consequences of mismanaging the environment and trade protectionism and are active voices in the fora discussing topics such as global warming and GATT (General Agreement on Tariffs and Trade).

240 The economic problems afflicting the Commonwealth's poor are prevalent elsewhere but some have a special intensity and focus in the Commonwealth. Already, struggling to feed their people, several of the lowest income Commonwealth nations can expect annual population growth of three per cent and upwards between now and the end of the century. They include Kenya, at 3.9 per cent the fastest growing low income nation monitored by the World Bank, followed by Zambia (3.5 per cent), Tanzania (3.4 per cent), Uganda (3.3 per cent), Pakistan (3.3 per cent), Ghana (3.1 per cent) and Nigeria (3.0 per cent).

241 In most cases these projections show a marginal fall in the rate of population growth these countries have experienced in the 1980s. But during the past decade they have, with the exception of Pakistan, also shown a fall in GNP per capita growth. In the larger group of 13 Commonwealth countries represented in the bracket characterised by the World Bank as low-income, only five (Uganda, India, Pakistan, Nigeria and Ghana) managed to increase the measure of per capita food production in the first three-quarters of the 1980s.

242 It is not then surprising that life expectancy at birth in the Commonwealth's poorest countries is around the mid-50s – some 20 years less than that for the citizens of the Commonwealth's industrialised nations. This statistic correlates with the lower proportion of low income countries' budgets spent on health services (between two and six per cent) compared to the proportion (six to 13 per cent) allocated by their richer Commonwealth partners.

243 Sadly too in several of the Commonwealth's poorest countries government spending on education has been falling – in some cases, it has nearly halved as a proportion of their total budgets in the past 20 years. For many, an obvious factor has been the competition with demands for growing defence and debt servicing budgets.

244 The rise in defence spending at the expense of social services is a grim reminder that some of the Commonwealth's poorest nations experience border conflict as well as civil security problems. For example the proportion of government spending allocated to defence rose between 1972 and 1987 while proportionate spending on education, housing and social security fell over the same period in Bangladesh, Tanzania and Sri Lanka. The same situations that produce such switches in resources also give rise to dislocated communities and associated homelessness and refugees in the Asian sub-continent and in Africa.

245 The debt burden of developing countries was brought dramatically to the world's attention by Latin America in the early 1980s. This subject has been exhaustively researched and there have been several generations of proposals for dealing with it. The best known deal with relaxation of the terms and repayment of commercial debt. Some debt-burdened Commonwealth borrowers, such as Jamaica and Nigeria, have taken advantage of new techniques that arrange to swap their debt obligations for direct investment (i.e. shares) in commercial enterprises. By doing so debt-servicing charges are reduced while equity investment becomes entrenched.

246 In addition to those debtors, there is a group of even more distressed borrowers whose need for assistance extends to the servicing and repayment of the concessional loans they have obtained from multilateral banks. Commonwealth countries feature prominently among this group in which a 25 per cent debt service ratio (the ratio of export receipts to interest changes on external debt) is typically used as the qualifying criterion. At the same time, 26 of the 43 developing nations in the Commonwealth have been able to access the international capital markets in the past decade, although the regular borrowers number only about half a dozen.

247 Despite their success in adjusting and developing their institutions, developing countries face new problems in the competition for capital that will increase as Eastern Europe's

development gathers pace. Already there is evidence that shrinking bank lending (even against trade) has forced developing countries to resort to barter and countertrade. The materials they have at hand to effect such transactions are frequently commodities whose prices are volatile. Even where such commodities are exported for cash, they are an unpredictable source of income. An analysis of 37 Commonwealth developing countries' exports shows that coffee accounts for more than a third of export receipts in four of them, sugar for a similar proportion in a further five, and cocoa for upwards of ten per cent in a further four. Nor have the international agreements between producers and their main customers, designed to regulate the prices of such commodities, proved capable of smoothing the balance of supply and demand for them. Others are substantially dependent on spices, coconut products, tobacco, copper, aluminium, bauxite and timber.

248 These raw goods along with typical manufactures such as textiles, clothing and leather goods also face a sophisticated range of protectionist measures as they attempt to penetrate export markets – including the markets of some of their industrialised Commonwealth partners. Indeed, it has been estimated that the costs of such protectionism in terms of lost market, price distortions and resultant employment are twice the aid flows into such developing countries.

Chapter 11

THE ENVIRONMENT

249 Since the 1970s, there has been a steady growth in awareness that the natural world might be experiencing irreversible damage, which could in turn threaten the future of human life itself. It is possible to trace the international growth and changing nature of this concern. Member states of the Commonwealth have made many contributions to alleviating difficulties and this section of the Report sets them against this background. It also assesses the potential which exists for achieving greater international understanding and co-operation in the future.

Worldwide concern about the environment

250 Early warnings about the exploitation of the earth were concerned mostly with the depletion of resources, particularly minerals. Some of the most influential predictions were published in 1972. In that year *Blueprint for Survival*, shortly followed by the Club of Rome's *Limits to Growth*, warned that if contemporary rates of population growth and consumption of food and non-renewable materials were maintained, the limits of future growth would be reached within the very near future. It was predicted that before the year 2000 there would be a desperate land shortage with accompanying soil erosion as unsuitable land was brought into cultivation. Known reserves of tin would be exhausted within 17 years (from 1972), petroleum in 31 years and copper in 36 years. The extent to which natural systems would be able to absorb pollution was very variable but not infinite and in some situations had already been exceeded. Long before this stage, however, it would be likely that competition for rapidly diminishing resources would result in social upheaval, and possibly war.

251 Falling fertility rates, greater agricultural yields and more careful use of resources meant the revision of these gloomy predictions. Nevertheless, the alarms served a useful purpose. The earlier

predictions might have been fulfilled if concern had not been expressed about population and resource levels and action taken.

252 In the same year, 1972, the United Nations set up an International Conference on the Human Environment in Stockholm which was attended by delegates from over 90 countries. This was also concerned with the exploitation of the natural world but many less developed countries, wishing to raise their standards of living through increased economic prosperity, regarded international pressures for conservation with suspicion, as being inimical to their development.

253 *North-South: A programme for Survival* (The Brandt Report), which was published in 1980, devoted little attention to conservation matters as such. It expressed concern at the rate of depletion of natural resources, and at the levels of pollution. It also recognised the difficulties of building environmental costs into economic equations. The proposals of the Brandt Report, if substantially implemented, could have had far-reaching consequences for the environment. By alleviating poverty, people in poorer countries might have been prevented from adopting those measures which ensure short-term survival at the expense of long-term environmental degradation.

254 By 1980, concern about the environment had broadened considerably. The loss of agricultural soils, pressures on water supplies for drinking, agriculture and industry, and pollution presented problems for many countries. Associated with these was the realisation that many species of birds and plants had become extinct or were gravely at risk. Against this background, the International Union for the Conservation of Nature and Natural Resources, the World Wildlife Fund (now the World Wide Fund for Nature) and the United Nations Environment Programme launched a World Conservation Strategy. More than 450 agencies and 700 scientists from all parts of the world took part in the production of the Strategy, which was aimed at both maintaining and developing the capacity of the earth to support human life. It had three stated objectives:

To maintain the processes of the planet essential for sustaining all life.

To preserve as many varieties of plant and animal life as possible.

To ensure the sustainable use of natural resources by us and our children.

All countries were urged to prepare their own responses to the Strategy as a basis for further internal and international discussion.

Brundtland Commission

255 The most recent international initiative was the setting up by the United Nations General Assembly of the World Commission on Environment and Development in 1983. Chaired by Gro Brundtland, the then Prime Minister of Norway, it was required to re-examine the critical environmental and development problems of the planet, to formulate realistic proposals for their solution, and to ensure that human progress could be sustained without prejudicing the wellbeing of future generations. The Introduction to the Commission's report, *Our Common Future*, included the following:

> Our report is not a prediction of ever-increasing environmental decay, poverty, and hardship in an ever more polluted world among ever-decreasing resources. We see instead the possibility for a new era of economic growth, one that must be based on policies that sustain and expand the environmental resource base. And we believe such growth to be absolutely essential to relieve the great poverty that is deepening in much of the developing world.

But the Commission's hope for the future is conditional on decisive political action now to begin managing environmental resources to ensure both sustainable human progress and human survival.

256 This brief review of the worldwide growth of concern about the environment has not mentioned gatherings relating to specific issues such as desertification, hazardous wastes, or the use of chlorofluorcarbons (CFCs), or meetings of small groups of nations to discuss regional matters. What has been presented gives a brief outline of the increase in awareness of the deleterious effects on the natural world of much human activity, and a description of how the substance of the concern has changed over the last twenty years.

The role of the Commonwealth

257 Given this background, what is the role of the Commonwealth in the face of such problems? A significant statement was made by the first Secretary-General when he said that the Commonwealth could help member countries to 'learn how to share the planet'. In 1966, Macfarlane Burnet, the Chairman of the Board of the Trustees of the

Commonwealth Foundation, stated that one objective should be 'to foster the ideal of one world rather than to perpetuate the Commonwealth as a political unit'. This was echoed by Shridath Ramphal in his acceptance speech as Secretary-General in 1975, who anticipated the growing environmental crisis better than many, when he set out his picture of the Commonwealth as 'a forum for advancing the wider human dialogue on which our planetary survival may now depend'.

258 Different parts of the Commonwealth are subject to different environmental threats. It is largely true to say that until the 1980s, it was very easy for anyone living in one of the developed countries of the Commonwealth to assume that environmental problems affected people elsewhere in the world but were of little domestic significance. The damage to the ozone layer by CFCs used in aerosol sprays and refrigeration equipment, and the likely consequences of global warming have done much to make people in developed countries more aware of the fragility of the environment. It has also made them think more carefully about their use of energy and wasteful practices resulting in pollution.

259 However, as the Brundtland Report indicated, poverty generally leads to environmental degradation. In many developing countries, the imperatives of daily survival force poor families to think (and live) short-term – to overgraze grasslands, to overexploit soils to maximise immediate yields, to cut down dwindling forest stocks for farmland or firewood. What is, individually, rational behaviour becomes a collective disaster. The disaster is compounded by the pressure of population growth, which is often highest in the very countries doubly threatened by 'natural' environmental disasters and that of poverty. In Bangladesh, where almost every last acre of cultivable land is already used – and millions live precariously on mudbanks facing imminent disaster – the population is expected to double from 110 million to 220 million over the next 35 years, even if the birthrate halves over that period.

260 All less developed countries wish to increase their economic prosperity in order to raise living standards for their people. In environmental terms this may give rise to tensions. Calls from wealthier countries for limiting economic growth for the sake of environmental protection and resource conservation have been challenged by poorer nations who feel that their opportunities for

securing more of the world's resources and sharing in better standards of living are being restricted. Questions of population limitation are met with similar suspicion which has hindered constructive international discussions. It is in trying to resolve some of these difficulties that the Commonwealth has a significant part to play.

Commonwealth Forestry Association

261 Several Commonwealth initiatives on the environment already exist. One of the longest standing, the Commonwealth Forestry Association, was set up in 1921 as The Empire Forestry Association. This was responsible for the creation of the Commonwealth (formerly Imperial) Forestry Institute at the University of Oxford. The complex of organisations associated together in the CFI provide a centre for postgraduate education, research into problems of tropical forestry, post-experience training, advice, information and communication. All these elements are designed expressly to assist in development.

262 Forestry in its broadest sense is central to many of the environmental land issues of the developing world – the wise management of tropical rain forest lands, the fight against desertification, preventing the erosion of mountain catchments, meeting the need for fuel wood, wildlife conservation and national park management. On the good management of forest lands depend food and wood and much else besides.

Food production

263 There is also long standing co-operation between countries on matters relating to food production. A conference on agricultural research in 1927 recommended the creation of agencies to disseminate information about different subjects throughout the Empire. Eight Agricultural Bureaux were set up to deal with subjects such as soil science, animal genetics and fruit production.

264 A more recent development has been the creation of the Food and Rural Development Division of the Commonwealth Secretariat. This is concerned with increasing agricultural output while at the same time having regard to sustainable use of the environment. It has prime responsibility for managing the Commonwealth programme to assist African countries in sustainable development. Commonwealth

leaders meeting at Vancouver in 1987 welcomed the Secretariat's study, *Conservation for Sustainable Development*, which focused on the scope for Commonwealth action to counteract soil erosion, desertification and drought in Africa. They asked the Secretary-General to implement its recommendations through a long-term programme, co-ordinated by the Secretariat in partnership with countries in the region and supported by other Commonwealth members.

Expert group on Climate Change and Sea Level Rise

265 In April 1987, a storm surge caused unprecedented damage to the Maldives, particularly to its capital, Malé. This was followed by two extraordinary swells at high tide. These events would have been largely ignored by the rest of the world had the President of the Maldives not brought them to the attention of the Commonwealth and of the United Nations. His message was that there is growing anxiety among some islands, and other low-lying states, that fundamental and irreversible changes are taking place in the world's climate and sea level. At Vancouver, in 1987, Commonwealth Heads of Government realised that this problem had other dimensions. The President of Bangladesh, a country that has experienced a succession of enormously destructive floods, urged the necessity of looking at the underlying environmental causes of flooding and natural disasters.

266 These concerns led to the establishment of a ten-member Commonwealth Expert Group on Climate Change and Sea Level Rise, with Commonwealth-wide membership and expertise, under the Chairmanship of Dr Martin Holdgate, the Director-General of the International Union for the Conservation of Nature. The Commonwealth in selecting membership of its Expert Groups is not subject to the same restrictions imposed on other international bodies such as the United Nations, where care has to be taken to ensure that committees and working parties are fully representative.

267 The Expert Group prepared its report for Heads of Government meeting at Kuala Lumpur in 1989. Its work has been supported by the Australian Development Assistance Bureau which helped finance detailed case studies on the impact of sea-level rise on six low-lying states (Bangladesh, Guyana, Kiribati, Maldives, Tonga and Tuvalu), as well as some studies on the effect of sea-level changes on coral reefs and mangrove swamps.

268 The first task the group set itself was to study the scientific evidence for anticipated changes in the global climate. There is now a scientific consensus that global average temperatures are likely to rise by 1-2°C by the year 2030 and to continue to rise thereafter. While it is not possible to gauge climatic impacts more precisely there is an expectation that wet areas could become wetter and dry areas drier, that there could be susbstantial winter warming in high latitudes (in Canada, for example), and that the severity of tropical storms and hurricanes could increase. One specific consequence of this global warming is that the sea-level is also likely to rise – possibly by more than 20cm by the year 2030, and maybe higher. This is obviously a matter of serious concern to the low-lying Commonwealth countries already threatened by flooding and the intrusion of saltwater into water supplies. In particular, low-lying islands and other countries can anticipate an increase in the frequency of storm surges. Increased flooding in delta countries and others drained by large, slow-flooding rivers seems likely and is of particular concern to Bangladesh.

269 Although the environmental effects of global warming on individual countries cannot at this stage be predicted very clearly, the Group tried, as its second task, to predict the possible socio-economic repercussions. The consequences for natural ecosystems such as forests, coral reefs and mangrove swamps could be significant because of limits to their natural powers of adaption. A major concern exists, too, over long-term investment in areas sensitive to climate change such as water supplies, agricultural research, commercial forestry, hydro-power and sea defences. In general, developing countries, because of their greater dependence on natural systems, will have to adapt most but with fewer resources.

270 The Expert Group also looked at policy implications, particularly the need to reduce 'greenhouse gas' emissions in a way that is consistent with the need for growth in developing countries.

Langkawi Declaration on the Environment

271 The report from the Commonwealth Expert Group on Climate Change and Sea Level Rise together with many other initiatives which involve small groupings of states within the Commonwealth, prompted the Heads of Government at their meeting in 1989 to issue the Langkawi Declaration on the Environment. This recognised the

dangers from environmental degradation together with its causes, and expressed a commitment to work together and separately to find better ways of integrating environmental dimensions in economic decision making, transferring technologies, and of supporting research on climate change and applying its findings. Clauses were also included which related to forests, ozone damaging substances, pollution, the disposal of hazardous wastes, and the need to maintain genetic diversity among animals and plants. The need for new international agreements was recognised.

Environmental issues and the Anglican Communion

272 The growth in awareness of the threats to the environment in the Commonwealth has also been displayed among the churches of the Anglican Communion, as can be demonstrated by an examination of the Lambeth Conference Proceedings. A concern was expressed in 1958 about the need to share the world's resources more equitably. This has broadened in scope with successive Conferences. The 1968 Lambeth Conference urged:

> all Christians, in obedience to the doctrine of creation, to take all possible action to ensure man's responsible stewardship over nature; in particular in his relationship with animals, and with regard to the conservation of soil, and the prevention of the pollution of air, soil and ocean.

The 1978 Conference recognised that:

> the people and the resources of the world are made by God and are therefore good: we are not to destroy them or waste them since he cares about them and so must we.

The Bishops addressed themselves to the need to eradicate world poverty and to this end, called upon world leaders and governments to establish a new economic order, aimed at securing fair prices for raw materials and manufactured goods, and reversing the process by which the rich become richer and the poor poorer.

273 In 1988, a complex resolution was accepted by the Bishops which linked together issues of justice and peace, militarism and the future sustainability of the environment. It called upon all Provinces and dioceses to devise a programme of study, reflection and action which should encompass the dissemination of information about what is happening to the environment. It should also lead people to ask questions about the environmental and social consequences of

economic policies and the exercise of power within and without the Church, and should urge people to review their lifestyles and to support other agencies which share concerns about the natural world. The report of the 1988 Conference stated that

> Christians must recognise that concern for the environment is concern for God's world both for its own sake and for the capacity of human beings to flourish in it. The world has come into being by the creative act of God and is therefore a gift to us to be revered and cared for as his, not ours. It may even be called our sacrament of creation, which is to be received and shared, enjoyed and celebrated, and used in such a way that its benefits can be passed on to our children. For this to occur, we must all recognise that we live in a highly sensitive, single, interlocking system which demands from all of humanity a high level of reverence, respect and responsibility. Together with all people of good will, Christians must learn again to cherish the God-given resources of the earth, through responsible stewardship of technology and of the environment.

Conclusion

274 The countries which are represented in the Commonwealth and in the Anglican Communion can offer one another practical assistance. In some cases, the help given is substantial – as shown by some of the schemes outlined above. In others, it is limited but no less valuable. So, for example, one English diocese works with an African diocese on a tree planting scheme. Beyond the practical, both the Commonwealth and the Anglican Communion offer countries the opportunity to engage in dialogue. This is vital if sustainable use of the earth is to be achieved. Wealthy countries cannot expect to enhance, or even maintain, their standards of living, based as they are on enormous consumption of natural resources, while asking poorer countries to implement conservation measures which would restrict their opportunities for growth, however limited they may be. The Langkawi Declaration is a significant step towards beginning this dialogue, for which there are no easy or quickly achieved solutions.

Chapter 12

SPORT

275 Nothing – not even the role of HM the Queen – gives the Commonwealth larger public attention than its very distinctive sporting connections. Large audiences are attracted locally to Test Matches and to Commonwealth Games, and television coverage brings these Commonwealth sporting occasions into the homes of countless millions across the globe.

276 It is worth emphasising one unique aspect of all of this. In a variety of ways the Commonwealth can be compared with the United Nations. Yet the UN has no association with international sport. In particular it has no links with the Olympic Games. By contrast the Commonwealth is intimately involved both with a considerable number of international sporting activities, and with the four-yearly Commonwealth Games. For very many people these are indeed much its most salient and important feature, and without them the Commonwealth would be very much the poorer.

Sport and political issues

277 Because of this interaction between sport and the Commonwealth, Commonwealth activities have periodically been caught up in some of the issues that have affected the Commonwealth politically. Departure or exclusion from the Commonwealth politically will almost certainly also entail exclusion from Commonwealth sporting connections. This is not a consequence which the much larger number of people than those who view the Commonwealth in essentially political terms take to at all kindly.

278 As we saw in Chapter 9, the most substantial of these has concerned sporting connections with, and political policies towards, South Africa. On these the Commonwealth has not only shown itself for the most part to be extraordinarily resolute but highly successful as well. Thanks to the Commonwealth's insistence, international

sporting connections with South Africa came almost universally to a halt – to the dismay of a great many of South Africa's sports-loving white population. A number of firm stands against these at the cost of the cancellation and boycott of several Commonwealth sporting occasions served to dramatise the widespread abhorrence of South Africa's apartheid policies in the Commonwealth and in the world at large. The key step in this direction was taken when Commonwealth Heads of Government in 1977 adopted the Gleneagles Agreement on Sporting Contacts with South Africa. There were those, not least in Britain, who viewed such decisions with a good deal of hostility – and in such quarters that did the Commonwealth's reputation no good – but very large numbers of others believed the price to be entirely well warranted.

The main sporting activities

279 A number of sports followed the expansion of the British Empire around the globe. In several Commonwealth countries these have now become entrenched as the principal source of public spectacle, public enjoyment and public involvement. In some instances a particular sport – cricket in the West Indies is a prime example – plays a major role both in meeting the aspirations of very many young people (and not so young too!) and in providing a degree of cohesion to otherwise disparate and even fragile societies. Cricket enjoys great public interest as well in Australia and in India and Pakistan and is growing in Sri Lanka. Rugby Football is followed widely in New Zealand, and in several of the island member countries of the South West Pacific such as Tonga, Fiji and Western Samoa. Rugby League has many adherents too. The high points for these sports lie in their intra-Commonwealth matches. For very many people discourse in a Commonwealth context is talk about sport. There are four principal ones.

280 Cricket has long been a major sport in a large number of Commonwealth countries. By the 1860s English cricket XIs started to tour in Canada, Australia, New Zealand and South Africa, and before 1900 were visiting India, Ceylon (as it then was) and the West Indies. An Imperial Cricket Conference was founded in 1909. During the first half of the twentieth century nothing became more important to cricket than its intra-Commonwealth Test Matches. Over the years

these have variously been dominated by English teams, by Australian teams, and by West Indian teams, but the Indian and Pakistan cricketers have been major figures, and New Zealand and Sri Lanka have played memorable cricket too. Since the 1970s 'World Cup' tournaments of one-day cricket which these Commonwealth countries dominate have come to be held, and, aside from their television audiences, have attracted very large crowds. Nearly 100,000, for example, have attended in Calcutta.

281 Rugby Football not only enjoys great public support in various parts of the British Isles, in Wales perhaps most particularly, but in Australasia and the South West Pacific. Commonwealth tours by the British Lions, the Australian Wallabies, the New Zealand All Blacks, and others, invariably constitute high points in a season's programme.

282 Hockey is important too. India was long its main star. It is notable that since its beginnings in 1908 Olympic hockey has only once not been won by a Commonwealth country (by West Germany in 1972). Its recent winners have included Britain, New Zealand and Pakistan, as well as India. In the last two it enjoys a considerable public following.

Commonwealth Games

283 Of all the Commonwealth sporting occasions none, however, is more important than the Commonwealth Games. After a variety of preliminaries the first British Empire Games were held in Canada in 1930. To begin with they were held between individuals, and not between countries, and first comprised athletics, bowls, rowing, swimming, diving and wrestling only. In 1932 a British Empire Games Federation was formed. In 1954 their name was changed to the British Empire and Commonwealth Games; in 1970 to the British Commonwealth Games, and finally in 1974 to, simply, the Commonwealth Games (now held every four years so as to alternate with the Olympic Games).

284 A characteristic high point came at the Vancouver games in 1954, the first to be televised, when Sir Roger Bannister (as he now is) from Britain and John Landy from Australia both bettered the 'four minute mile' in a race against each other. Thereafter African athletes came increasingly to the fore. In 1962 Seraphino Antao from Kenya won

both the 100 and 220 yards. By 1974 African countries were winning over 50 of the medals.

285 In 1986 32 countries boycotted the Edinburgh Games in protest against British policy concerning sanctions against South Africa. Thereafter, however, the Auckland Games in 1990 were the largest of all, with 55 countries competing (several smaller territories in the Commonwealth participate on their own behalf), and some 2,500 competitors all told. HM the Queen and members of the royal family now regularly attend, and the Commonwealth Secretary-General also.

286 Given the steeply rising cost, both in providing the most up-to-date training facilities, and in actually mounting the four-yearly Commonwealth Games, it was becoming clear, however, that there were significant issues to be considered if developing and especially smaller Commonwealth countries were not to be increasingly marginalised at the Games. This was highlighted by the decision to hold the 1994 Games, not in India which wanted them, but once again in Canada. Only in 1966 in Kingston, at the time of Jamaica's independence, have the Games been held anywhere other than in a 'white' country. In a seminal move the Commonwealth Secretary-General accordingly set up in 1990 a Working Party:

> to identify ways of strengthening Commonwealth sport ... to examine financial aspects, including the possible creation of a Commonwealth Sports Trust, ways in which the revenue-generating potential of the Games themselves might be enhanced, and how to ensure that the Games are held in all regions of the 50-member association.

It will report to the next Commonwealth Heads of Government meeting in Harare in October 1991.

287 This is a striking instance of the way in which the very much wider activities that embrace the Commonwealth than simply its political aspects are coming to be recognised. As the Commonwealth Games so palpably demonstrate, the Commonwealth is a Commonwealth of peoples and not just of governments, and as such has very few counterparts.

PART III

Chapter 13

A PLACE FOR HUMAN FLOURISHING

288 It has been said by Malcolm Fraser, former Prime Minister of Australia, that the Commonwealth is such a surprising and unique organisation that if it did not exist 'it would be impossible to invent it or even conceive it. For it would seem to violate or, better, transcend all our expectations of alignment between nations'. The first part of this quotation might also be applied to the Anglican Communion. Today the role of the Commonwealth is challenged ever more strongly by our new political and economic alignment with Europe; while the unity and fellowship of the autonomous Churches in the Anglican Communion are seriously under threat. While we ourselves approached our task with varying degrees of commitment to (and even understanding of) both Commonwealth and Anglican Communion, in sharing our knowledge and ideas, in hearing evidence and reading more widely, we have come to share a conviction that Britain has in the Commonwealth, and the Church of England in the Anglican Communion, rich and precious resources of which both nation and Church seem all too little aware.

289 In para. 2 we said our brief was

> to analyse the nature of the Commonwealth and Britain's past and present within it, and to ask if there are lessons to be learned from the analogous membership of the Church of England within the Anglican Communion: e.g. how bodies may be autonomous and interdependent; how communities may heal painful memories and redeem present tensions.

Such an analysis starts with self-knowledge. National characteristics cannot be wished away. Many have experienced the British as insular, stubborn, arrogant, prejudiced and xenophobic; but equally they can be brave, adventurous, tolerant, just and idealistic. Some of these contrasting characteristics both created and left their mark on the Empire, and are also clearly reflected in our religious history, not least in the traditions that were hammered out at the Reformation and which had such an an impact on the Church of England.

290 'It hath been the wisdom of the Church of England' states the Preface to the 1662 Book of Common Prayer, in what is a classic statement on the Anglican way, 'to keep the mean between the two extremes, of too much stiffness in refusing, and of too much easiness in admitting any variation from it ...' The Anglican Church has always contained people of diverse views, somehow holding them in an uncomfortable tension. What holds Anglicans together is an ethos, a way of looking at things, a certain way of life, worship and devotion. Its characteristics are worth noting:

> We are a deeply biblical Church, our worship and our spirituality reflected for so long in the Biblical and liturgical content and style of the Book of Common Prayer.
>
> We place great emphasis on the conscience of the individual believer. We affirm spiritual freedom and freedom of scholarship, with a strong appeal to reason.
>
> We are a comprehensive Church and value toleration, even tolerating for the time being what may appear erroneous. We allow wide interpretation of doctrine and theological speculation, valuing reticence, restraint and moderation over the easier role of partisanship. We accept that truth may often lie in both extremes.

On comprehensiveness, the 1988 Lambeth Conference Report had this to say:

> It is an attitude of mind which Anglicans learn from the thought-provoking controversies of their history. It demands agreement on fundamentals, while tolerating disagreement on matters in which Christians may differ without feeling the necessity of breaking communion. It is not compromise, nor a sophisticated word for syncretism. Rather it implies that the apprehension of truth is a growing thing.... and there must be a continuing search for the whole truth in which the Protestant and Catholic elements will find complete reconciliation.

291 It has been claimed that 'there is an Anglicanism which is of England and an Anglicanism which is of God,' overlapping but distinct – a claim some would contest. Even so the connection in England between Church and State, shaped by the turmoils of the sixteenth century, was used to preserve what was of God in Anglicanism and to take it to those lands where the Empire spread. But later, most of the Anglican connection with the English State had to be discarded, often painfully and gradually. Anglican Churches

have often had to lose their privileged position and their Englishness has had to be diminished before they truly took root. Yet the essential Anglican ethos was maintained within the fellowship of these autonomous provinces.

292 The central act of the Anglican Reformation had been the repudiation of a central authority: the belief that each national Church has the right to govern itself. In the nineteenth century, in the wake of Empire and of American independence, the Anglican Communion grew as a family of churches united in faith by their episcopal ministry and by their shared liturgy, but still acknowledging no over-riding authority. As Bishop Mark Santer has written:

> (This) principle of national or provincial sovereignty remained inviolate. This structure has been reinforced by the parallel development of the British Commonwealth of Nations. At the centre of Communion and Commonwealth alike there is a figure who is a personal focus of loyalty and who exercises considerable moral authority while possessed of no coercive power.

293 Nowhere has the tension so threatened the future of the Anglican Communion as over the question of the ordination of women as priests and bishops. That the Communion has not only held together, but emerged from the 1988 Lambeth Conference strengthened, was in part due to the role of the Archbishop of Canterbury. Lord Runcie visited during his tenure of office 22 of the 28 provinces and was held in high affection. He placed great importance on listening and moderation. He enabled the various parties to work things through, managing to hold together people of strongly diverse views. But it is also due to this peculiarly Anglican spirit, not of weak compromise, but of a toleration of views which at its best the Anglican Communion is able to contain in a dynamic and creative tension. In Lord Runcie's words: 'It is precisely in living with this tension that our tradition finds its particular genius and its distinctive contribution to the Catholic Church'. (At its worst, of course, it can be as perverse and lacking in vision as any other human institution.)

294 If, then, the Anglican Communion is in itself a sign and a model of how bodies may be both autonomous and interdependent (para. 132), it is worth affirming and celebrating. For the parallels with the Commonwealth are clear, and constructive analogies may be drawn concerning the potentially divisive issues of race, politics and economics. The question of women's ordination (or, in the

Commonwealth context, South Africa) should not be a scapegoat for all the issues with power to divide us, though it is a focus of them. In a paper to the assembled bishops at the 1988 Lambeth Conference, Elizabeth Templeton, the Church of Scotland theologian, spoke of what might be called 'communities of disagreement'. On the question of internal Anglican unity, and the tensions raised by matters of grave disagreement, she wrote:

> I have been constantly struck by the best generosity of your recurrent insistence that across parties, camps, styles and dogmas, you have need of one another. Both internally and in relation to other evolving Christian life forms, you have been conspicuously unclassifiable, a kind of ecclesiastical duck-billed platypus, robustly mammal *and* vigorously egg-laying. That, I am sure, is to be celebrated and not deplored.

295 In para. 129 we quote Mrs Templeton's words about seeing the issue of women's ordination as a gift. The quotation continues

> If it is gift, it is gift not just because it opens up deep and wide theological questions, but because it also touches the levels of pain and passion which test what it means that we love our enemies. The world is used to unity of all sorts ... unity in resistance, communities of party, creed, interest. But it is *not* used to such possibilities as this: that, for example, those who find the exclusion of women from the priesthood an intolerable apartheid and those who find their inclusion a violation of God's will *should enter into one another's suffering. Somewhere in there authority lies.* (Our italics)

296 This concept of 'gift' is central to our thinking. It is spoken of in para. 273 in terms of the creation, and in para. 128, where we write:

> ... The worldwide communion is a gift from God. Here is a possible key to using the inheritance of the past in a way that is creative for the future. Rather than seeing the Anglican Communion as an awkward encumbrance, as some do, many people in the Church of England have found it a gift to save us from an introverted and self-important preoccupation with our own affairs.

The same concept gives shape to Chapter 4 of this Report in which we argue that

> we might see (the Commonwealth) as a gift to the world of international affairs standing for the possibility of quality relationships which as a benefit – not a *raison d'être* – serve the interests of its partners. Things which partake of the quality of gift fit well with a Christian understanding of human life in relation to God. (para. 107)

297 It is one of the great insights of Orthodox Christianity that the

world has no meaning unless we see it as the sacrament of God's presence. For the writers of Genesis the creation is good, and in blessing it God makes the world the sign and means of his presence. Both the creation and life itself are God's gifts to his creatures. But gifts may be accepted responsibly and thankfully and shared; or taken for granted; or rejected and destroyed.

298 Central to Christianity is the belief that to live under God is to live eucharistically: taking what is given and thankfully offering it back to God. 'It is our duty and our joy, at all times and in all places, to give thanks....' Only then does the world recover its true meaning, when the value of what is given is recognised and affirmed. Hence the uniquely Christian understanding of 'gift' and our trusteeship of what is given is focused in the bread and wine of the Eucharist, which mediate Christ to us, not least by giving us a foretaste of the Kingdom of God. The Kingdom where all will share equally the resources of the earth, receiving what is given thankfully and, by sharing it, restoring its true meaning.

299 The Christian vision concerns the nature of what is truly human and we are committed to human well-being (paras 89 and 90) and how that is best protected and nurtured. With threats to the environment caused by depletion of the ozone layer, industrial pollution, deforestation, global warming and war, we are suddenly very conscious of the fragility of the earth. But it is not only in the Bible that humankind is seen as custodian, trustee of the good earth, deputising for God in the care of nature. The Qur'an clearly does so too. Muslims seek to approach the universe with an awed consecration which matches the Christian sense of a sacramental universe. So the concept of life as gift is a deep human insight that may be found among those of other faiths or none.

300 If the concept of 'gift' is central to our thinking, then so is the concept of being required to 'enter one another's suffering' (para. 295). To do so within the Anglican Communion, on such a divisive issue as the ordination of women as priests, will help to give us credibility as those whose mission is the healing of the nations, and not least in overcoming the dehumanising forms of racism and poverty in all its destructive forms. In para. 130 we quote important words from the Eames Commission on Communion and Women in the Episcopate:

> If those who find the *exclusion* of women from the priesthood and episcopate contrary to an understanding of God's justice and the meaning of the Incarnation, and those who find their *inclusion* an unacceptable development of the apostolic ministry, can come together to share each other's burdens and sufferings, then the Anglican Communion will have learned something of the meaning of communion with the God who suffers. And we shall have something to say about the unity of Christians and the unity of all humankind.

301 In terms of the Commonwealth, such healing will always have to begin with a healing of memories. We must penetrate *behind* what divides us to understand its nature. That calls for honesty and empathy, leading to penitence and forgiveness. But forgiveness does not mean forgetting, but the deliberate recalling of it and the accepting of responsibility for the way it was. Scar tissue is significant and important. 'Only by accepting the past' wrote T.S. Eliot, 'can we alter its meaning'. And whether that means the tracing back of the racism that afflicts us still in Britain to the paternalism of our imperialist past, or taking time to understand the anger on both sides of the women priests divide, it is necessarily painful and costly. But it will then be a creative costliness. As costly as the attempt by an Archbishop of Canterbury, working with the Anglican Primates or the Bishops gathered each decade at Lambeth, to influence and hold together culturally divergent provinces so that they are authentically Latin American or authentically African, while maintaining an authentically Anglican spirit, Catholic and Reformed, flexible yet united in the essentials of the Gospel.

302 The rejection of the Papal power by the Church of England at the Reformation was one act in a drama in which national identities were once again defined against the centralisation of religious power. The Church of England became the Church of the English people and developed particular insights, particular ways of approaching truth and tolerating dissentient and opposed views, that it exported along with Empire, commerce and cricket.

303 David Edwards, Provost of Southwark, has written:

> There will always be an England unless it is desertified by carbon dioxide or becomes an extension of the Arctic Circle, but for the forseeable future its economic and political destiny appears to be in membership (however reluctant) of the union of the states of Europe, and the era when it left Europe in order to rule a quarter of the human race will seem one with the imperial history of Egypt, Assyria and Babylon.

But it does not follow that the insights which Anglicanism has developed, or the truths for which the Commonwealth stands, will disappear. Both Church and Empire have had to adapt to the culture in which they were established: sometimes easily and naturally, sometimes radically, even bloodily. Christians have to proclaim the Gospel within a particular culture: political and economic systems need to be adapted to the needs of people as their history develops. Those truths and insights that are primary and fundamental must be preserved, but the forms in which they are expressed will change, and we should expect and welcome developing insights (through *perestroika* or the Holy Spirit, a fresh understanding – for example – of the place of women or the evil of the domination of one race or culture by another).

304 We do not doubt the 'provisional' nature of the Anglican Communion (para. 120). The best sort of Anglicanism looks beyond itself, sees itself as incomplete, always looking towards a wider unity. In 1954 Bishop Stephen Bayne, the first executive officer of the Anglican Communion, wrote:

> The vocation of Anglicanism is, ultimately, to disappear. That is its vocation precisely because Anglicanism does not believe in itself but it believes only in the Catholic Church of Christ; therefore it is for ever restless until it finds its place in that one body.

Many years before, in the *Gospel and the Catholic Church*, Bishop Michael Ramsey had written:

> While the Anglican Church is vindicated by its place in history, with a strikingly balanced witness to Gospel and Church and sound learning, its greater vindication lies in its pointing through its own history to something of which it is a fragment. Its credentials are its incompleteness, with the tension and travail in its soul. It is clumsy and untidy, it baffles neatness and logic. For it is sent not to commend itself as 'the best type of Christianity', but by its very brokenness to point to the universal Church wherein all have died.

305 Six years previously the 1930 Lambeth Conference had used similar words about the vocation of Anglicanism:

> Viewed in its widest relations, the Anglican Communion is in some sense an incident in the history of the church universal... In its present character we believe that it is transitional, and we forecast the day when the racial and historical connections which at present characterise it will be transcended, and the life of our Communion will be merged in a larger fellowship in the Catholic Church.

306 The Commonwealth has undergone change, and therefore this theme of 'provisionality' may have some usefulness in this context as well. The racial and historical connections which have characterised it (and still do to a great extent) may very well be equally transcended in a world in transition. 'Provisionality' is the recognition that your present condition has to do with the cultural context of a past or passing age: that it is temporary, not permanent. What matters is that the insights developed during the expansion of the Anglican Communion, and during the fruitful transformation of Empire into Commonwealth, are not lost. For the world has need of them. The Anglican Communion's role may be to bring to a fully united (though far from uniform) Church of God its own ethos, its Catholic-Evangelical axis, its equal emphasis on word and sacrament, its forbearance and toleration in its search for truth. Equally, the family of the Commonwealth has gathered from its history and manifests by its very diversity particular strengths and gifts to bring to the greater family of nations in tackling the ideological and economic issues of the next decade.

307 As became clear in our studies of rich and poor, the world is entering a new phase of how it divides politically and economically: Europe; the Americas/Canada; Japan/South East Asia. Increasingly this leaves the poor world marginalised. In such a world, it is only in the Commonwealth context that Africa and the Caribbean can sit down on equal terms with Canada and Australia, sharing their hugely different perceptions and insights. The Commonwealth will continue to have a significant voice in urging a more equitable approach to the problems of the poor nations – not least in strongly urging the major powers to take a more realistic and accommodating position with regard to debt. 'Must we starve our children to pay our debts?' Julius Nyerere, former President of Tanzania, has asked.

308 Some economists would claim that banks and governments in the developed world have encouraged their former colonies to mortgage their people's future with endless loans; that the suffering of peoples in the Third World is to some extent a basic prerequisite for our relative economic prosperity. The strongest nations are increasingly imposing their will, not in a new colonialism, but in economic pressures, and the poor countries face neglect and indifference while the rich get on with making money. Paul Vallely has described how for every pound that we send to the Third World

as aid, we recoup more than £2 through the tariffs and duties we impose on the raw materials they sell us. The Third World, according to 1990 World Bank figures, shelled out some 52 trillion dollars more in debt repayments than it received in aid. The United States administration has spoken recently of writing down the value of debt; while President Mitterrand has abolished the debt of a significant number of low income countries. There is a strong case for Britain, as part of the Commonwealth, to argue strongly for such changes (para. 233).

309 In our chapter on the Commonwealth, we emphasise the importance of Non-Government Organisations (para. 51ff), which have a special contribution to make in the areas concerning control of the population explosion, the promotion of human rights, the support of democratic processes, the spread of scientific and technical awareness, development education (especially in the rural areas), protection of the environment and the needs of small states. We believe it would be valuable if representatives of NGOs were present, perhaps with observer status, at all major meetings of the Governmental Commonwealth. We would also like to see the British Government encouraged to increase its funding to NGOs, especially the Commonwealth Foundation (para. 54), through the Commonwealth Secretariat; and not least to enlarge the work of its new Human Rights Unit.

310 We would hope for a greatly increased emphasis on imaginative education about the Commonwealth in schools and places of further education to go alongside teaching about the European Community. Here is a forum in which a number of critical issues can be addressed: racism, sexism, the gap between the 'haves' and the 'have nots', development and the environment. As we stated in para. 105:

> This unique relationship offers Britain an opportunity to press the case of the poor within the other communities of power of which she is a part – the EC and the special relationships with the USA.

311 The Commonwealth has proved, and could increasingly become, a place for human flourishing. But it is fragile, and once it is torn it is hard to restore. It will survive without Britain's active support, but how ironic if what grew from the ashes of the Empire, and still contains so much of the British spirit, should now be downgraded or dismissed. Few things are more potentially damaging to its structure than the introduction of full-cost fees for students from

abroad – first by Britain, now by certain parts of Canada and by Australia and New Zealand – leading to a drastic drop in students from the poorer Commonwealth countries. We draw particular attention to what we have written on Commonwealth Student Mobility (Chapter 6, para. 153). Tuition fees for overseas students have continued to rise sharply, and the number of Commonwealth students hosted in the four Commonwealth developed countries has fallen in five years, in marked contrast to the strongly promoted growth in international student mobility in countries like Germany, Japan and the United States. A policy which keeps the students of the Commonwealth developing countries away from the longer-established universities of the Commonwealth is uncommonly short-sighted, not least in terms of future contracts for the donor country.

312 As we have continually stressed, the Commonwealth is a modest international agency. We do not make exaggerated claims for it. We are aware of its faults. Its essential meaning is not about the gaining of power. Yet we believe it stands for good and wholesome values and is an agency for human well-being. It will, of course, survive, with or without our support. Yet it seems clear that one of the very considerable regrets in parts of the Commonwealth in recent years has been Britain's perceived refusal to continue to play a leading part in that moral leadership of the Commonwealth which she has provided in the past. From all we have seen the way stands open for her to stop sniping and take a lead once again in this unique world-wide association to which she has in the past contributed so substantially. There would be everything to be said for taking this opportunity, and nothing for its spurning.

BIBLIOGRAPHY

D. Adamson, *The Last Empire: Britain and the Commonwealth*, London: I.B. Tauris 1989

Dennis Austin, *The Commonwealth and Britain*, London: Routledge and Kegan Paul 1988

John Chadwick, *The Unofficial Commonwealth: the Story of the Commonwealth Foundation 1965-1980*, London: Allen and Unwin 1982

Stephen Chan, *The Commonwealth in World Politics: A Study of International Action 1965-1985*, London: Lester Crook Academic Publishing 1988

Commonwealth Secretariat, *The Commonwealth at the Summit: Communiqués of Commonwealth Heads of Government Meetings 1944-1985*, London: Commonwealth Secretariat 1987

Sir William Dale, *The Modern Commonwealth*, London: Butterworth 1983

Margaret Doxey, *The Commonwealth Secretariat and the Contemporary Commonwealth*, London: Macmillan 1989

A.J.R. Groom and Paul Taylor, *The Commonwealth in the 1980s: Challenges and Opportunities*, London: Macmillan 1984

John Howe, *Anglicanism and the Universal Church: Highways and Hedges 1958-1984 with an overview 1984-1990 (Colin Craston)* Anglican Book Centre Toronto 1990

Denis Judd and Peter Slinn, *The Evolution of the Modern Commonwealth 1902-1980*, London: Macmillan 1982

Nicholas Mensergh, *The Commonwealth Experience*, London: Weidenfeld and Nicolson, 2nd edition, 2 vols., 1983

W. David McIntyre, *The Significance of the Commonwealth 1965-1990*, London: Macmillan 1991

Trevor McDonald, *The Queen and the Commonwealth*, London: Thames Methuen 1986

S. Ramphal, *One World to Share: Selected Speeches of the Commonwealth Secretary-General 1975-9*, London: Hutchinson Benham 1979

Arnold Smith, *Stitches in Time: the Commonwealth in World Politics*, London: Andre Deutsch 1981

H.W. Springer, *The Commonwealth of Universities: the Story of the Association of Commonwealth Universities 1963-1988*, London: ACU 1988

Mission to South Africa: The Findings of the Commonwealth Eminent Persons Group on Southern Africa, Harmondsworth: Penguin Books 1986

Prisoners of Hope Report by the Board for Social Responsibility, London: CHP 1986

South Africa: the Sanctions Report, London: Penguin Books 1989

The Truth Shall Make You Free. The Lambeth Conference 1988, London: CHP 1988

The Round Table. The Commonwealth Journal of International Affairs, Abingdon: Carfax Publishing Company, quarterly.

COMMONWEALTH COUNTRIES

	Country	**Capital**	**Population**	
1	Antigua & Barbuda	St Johns	84,000	M
2	Australia	Canberra	16,506,000	M
3	Bahamas	Nassau	247,000	M
4	Bangladesh	Dhaka	108,851,000	R
5	Barbados	Bridgetown	255,000	M
6	Belize	Belmopan	182,000	M
7	Botswana	Gaborone	1,164,000	R
8	Britain	London	57,019,000	M
9	Brunei Darussalam	Bandar Seri Begawan	243,000	M*
10	Canada	Ottawa	26,104,000	M
11	Cyprus	Nicosia	686,000	R
12	Dominica	Roseau	81,000	R
13	The Gambia	Banjul	822,000	R
14	Ghana	Accra	14,040,000	R
15	Grenada	St George's	102,000	M
16	Guyana	Georgetown	799,000	R
17	India	Delhi	813,990,000	R
18	Jamaica	Kingston	2,429,000	M
19	Kenya	Nairobi	23,021,000	R
20	Kiribati	Tarawa	67,000	R
21	Lesotho	Maseru	1,673,000	M*
22	Malawi	Lilongwe	8,155,000	R
23	Malaysia	Kuala Lumpur	16,921,000	M*
24	Maldives	Malé	203,000	R
25	Malta	Valletta	345,000	R
26	Mauritius	Port Louis	1,048,000	M
27	Namibia	Windhoek	1,262,000	R
28	Nauru	Nauru	8,000	R
29	New Zealand	Wellington	3,339,000	M
30	Nigeria	Abuja	110,131,000	R
31	Pakistan	Islamabad	105,677,000	R
32	Papua New Guinea	Port Moresby	3,804,000	M

	Country	Capital	Population	
33	St Kitts & Nevis	Basseterre	43,000	M
34	St Lucia	Castries	145,000	M
35	St Vincent	Kingstown	122,000	M
36	Seychelles	Victoria	68,000	R
37	Sierra Leone	Freetown	3,938,000	R
38	Singapore	Singapore	2,639,000	R
39	Solomon Islands	Honiara	304,000	M
40	Sri Lanka	Colombo	16,565,000	R
41	Swaziland	Mbabane	737,000	M*
42	Tanzania	Dodoma	24,739,000	R
43	Tonga	Nuku'alofa	101,000	M*
44	Trinidad & Tobago	Port of Spain	1,241,000	R
45	Tuvalu	Funafuti	9,000	M
46	Uganda	Kampala	16,195,000	R
47	Vanuatu	Port Vila	151,000	R
48	Western Samoa	Apia	168,000	R
49	Zambia	Lusaka	7,486,000	R
50	Zimbabwe	Harare	9,257,000	R

M Monarchy under Queen Elizabeth II
M* Country with its own monarchy
R Republic
Population: mid-1988 figures, World Bank and Commonwealth Secretariat